So-ASN-374

Passport

To Your National Parks® Companion Guide

National Capital Region

Your Complete Guide to Cancellation Stamp Collecting

Randi Minetor

OCT 2008

FALCONGUIDES®

GUILFORD, CONNECTICUT
HELENA, MONTANA

AN IMPRINT OF THE GLOBE PEQUOT PRESS

FALCONGUIDES®

Text design by Nancy Freeborn
Maps by Tim Kissel © Morris Book Publishing, LLC

Library of Congress Cataloging-in-Publication Data is available on file.

ISBN: 978-0-7627-4510-4

Printed in the United States of America
10 9 8 7 6 5 4 3 2 1

Contents

917.5304 M662p 2008
Minetor, Randi.
Passport to your national
parks companion guide.

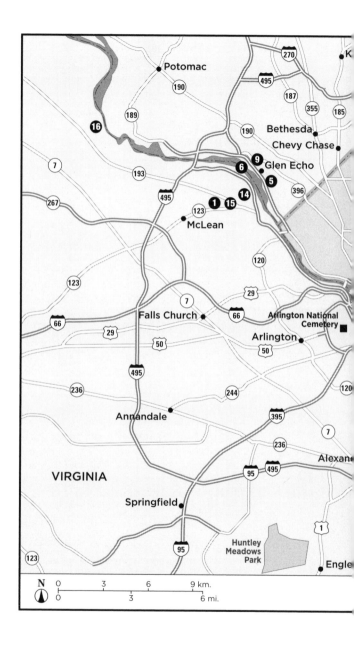

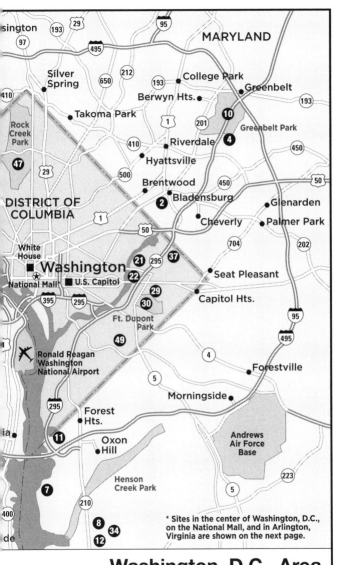

Washington, D.C., Area

* Sites in the center of Washington, D.C., on the National Mall, and in Arlington, Virginia are shown on the next page.

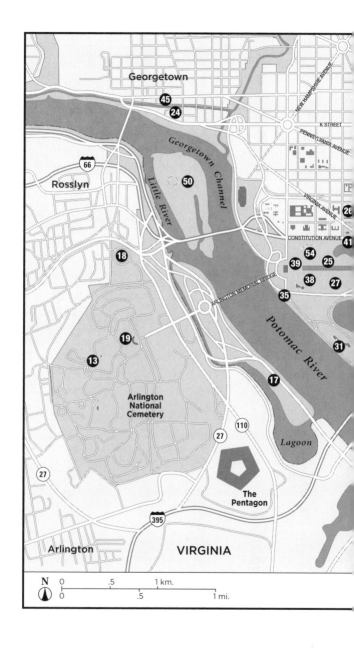

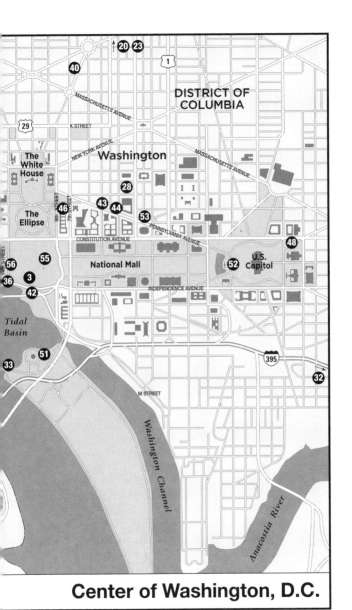

Center of Washington, D.C.

Preface

Friends and fellow Passport To Your National Parks® collectors have asked me why I took on the enormous project of creating a guidebook for my favorite hobby—an endeavor that has become a wonderful and endlessly fascinating part of my husband's and my life over the last seven years.

The need for this book hit me squarely between the eyes on a steamy August evening in 2002, when we stood in an empty Montana parking lot gazing at an inconspicuous green sign not 10 feet away that sealed our fate: PARK OPEN 8:30 A.M. TO 7:30 P.M. CENTRAL TIME.

Just across the state line in North Dakota stood the Fort Union Trading Post National Historic Site, our early evening destination, all rustic and inviting . . . and closed. Despite my calling ahead to check the closing time, despite the 90 miles of virtually empty road we'd traveled, and despite our fine planning . . . we had failed in our quest to collect our Passport cancellation.

Where had we gone wrong?

Nic and I had driven to North Dakota from our upstate New York home on an extended loop road trip that took the three of us—including June, my mother-in-law—to eleven official National Park sites across South and North Dakota, Montana, and Wyoming. For most people, such a trip through the scenic wonders of America's western prairie—the Badlands, the Black Hills, Wind and Jewel Caves, and the cataclysmic volcanic rupture that created Devils Tower—would be thrilling enough . . . but Nic and I traveled for a higher purpose. We were driven by our determination to collect Passport To Your

National Parks® cancellations at every park—and in some cases, to collect three, four, even five or more in one stop.

We'd hiked the rambling, wildflower-strewn quarry at Pipestone National Monument in Minnesota, descended more than 300 steps into the claustrophobic passageways of South Dakota's Wind Cave, and sat with thousands of spectators on benches in the late evening half-light to see Mount Rushmore's faces cast into shadows. We'd imagined Richard Dreyfuss's famed *Close Encounters of the Third Kind* mashed-potato sculpture of Devils Tower while standing at the base of its real-life counterpart, and we'd listened, enraptured, as a National Park Ranger revealed the irony in General Custer's ill-conceived battle at Little Bighorn. At every stop, we began our visit at the park bookstore, where we stamped our Passport book to commemorate the day. We came to get the cancellation, but we stayed because of the wonders we found.

Now in the home stretch, we had swooped down to the North Unit of Theodore Roosevelt National Park to get the Passport cancellation before the visitor center closed at 4:30 P.M., then made the drive back through the grasslands to Fort Union. On the way, I pulled out my mobile phone and called Fort Union to double-check the closing time. "Seven-thirty P.M.," the ranger confirmed. Not for one moment would it have occurred to me to respond with another question: "In which time zone?"

A funny thing happens to the time zone line in North Dakota. It zigzags along the edges of a dozen counties and through the middle of several, making the correct time a mystery to any unsuspecting traveler. Roughly following the path of the Missouri River, the time zone line even confuses some residents, who set their clocks to central time even though their neighborhoods are officially in mountain time.

So there was no way for us to know that in the top northwestern corner of the state, the time zone line veers sharply west, then follows the state border straight up to Canada.

We cruised up the long drive to the fort itself, enjoying the light of early evening as it turned the prairie the color of maple syrup. Then all three of us gasped at once. A tiny sign read: PARK OPEN 8:30 A.M. TO 7:30 P.M. CENTRAL TIME.

We looked at our watches. It was 6:45 P.M. mountain time . . . 7:45 P.M. central time.

Normal, sane travelers who had not been bitten by the Passport To Your National Parks® bug would have shrugged and driven away, skipping the fort altogether or leaving it for another vacation. We, however, schlepped back to Fort Union two days later to collect our cancellation, while Nic's mom sat in the back seat, counted yellow-headed blackbirds in the open fields, and chuckled at our misguided quest. The 97-mile back-track and hour-long visit to the fort—which turned out to be a charming fur-trading post with a droll mercenary perspective on the settlement of the Old West—set our trip back almost a full day.

On the return trip to Fort Union, Nic said casually, "If you're ever going to write another book, it should be a guide to the Passport program—so we never get stuck like this again."

This is that book.

The Passport program opens the door to magical moments and experiences you'll remember for a lifetime. With this book, you'll spend more time enjoying the parks and traveling to new places because you'll know exactly where to collect your Passport To Your National Parks® cancellations. I'm so pleased to have the opportunity to share this grand adventure with you and the hundreds of thousands of Passport cancellation collectors throughout the country. Enjoy your journey. Perhaps, on some distant mountain, in the recesses of a subterranean cavern, or in a visitor center in the nation's heartland, we'll meet and share our stories. I'll look forward to seeing all of your cancellations!

Acknowledgments

No project of this magnitude can come together unless many hands and minds join to make it happen—and I have literally hundreds of people to thank for their roles in bringing these field guides to bookshelves across America. In this limited space, I will acknowledge just a few of these helpful, encouraging, and supportive individuals.

First, I cannot say enough about the patient and persevering Scott Adams, executive editor for The Globe Pequot Press, the production team including Tracy Salcedo-Chourré and Shelley Wolf, and my extraordinary agent, Regina Ryan, for supporting this project from the beginning and seeing it through many channels and challenges over many months to bring about its eventual birth. Likewise, I thank Jason Scarpello and Chesley Moroz of Eastern National for their willingness to participate in this next extension of the Passport To Your National Parks® program. Rachel Shumsky and, later, Eileen Cleary at Eastern National maintained the list of Passport cancellation stamps at Eastern National's retail Web site, www.eparks.com, and they were quick to provide additional information when I needed it.

Many fellow Passport cancellation collectors were generous with their time and knowledge as I tackled the daunting task of pinpointing locations for every known, documented, and active cancellation in the country. Nancy Bandley's amazing National Park Travelers Club Master List was a tremendous tool, and I thank her for the use of this excellent information source. I am particularly grateful to my Internet friend John D. Giorgis, whose encyclopedic knowledge of the national parks system and his own adventurous travel tales were of great help—I do hope that John succeeds in his dream of becoming Secretary of the Interior one day. Dan Elias, Charlie and Rett Davenport-Raspberry, Greg Parkes, and Coleen Tighe all offered information and assistance, and I can't thank them enough for their insights.

Hundreds of national park and national heritage area rangers, staff members, supervisors, and volunteers answered my questions and took the time to return my calls, find facts, track down old cancellations, and verify new ones for me, often providing new kernels of information about their sites and the activities and lessons available at each. My respect for the National Park Service grew with each passing day as I connected with these well informed, gracious, and helpful people across the country. I thank all of them for their guidance, assistance, comments, and recommendations about the Passport program, as well as for their unfailing cheerfulness. In particular, I thank my old friend Rita St. John Gunther, a park ranger in the National Capital area, who went out of her way to determine the existence of a particularly recalcitrant cancellation.

Here at home, I would be struggling through the final fact-checking to this day if not for my devoted and uncomplaining assistant, Dan O'Donnell, who followed up with every park and property and checked every cancellation's availability. To Martin Winer, my "writing date" buddy and lifelong friend, I am grateful for the long afternoons we passed with laptops and java in coffeehouses and sandwich shops throughout Rochester while each of us worked on our separate projects. There is nothing better than a friend who knows when to talk and when to just let be.

Finally, to my husband, Nic, the love of my life and the man who opened up this world of travel for me by sharing his passion for the two-lane blacktop, and then by discovering the Passport program and launching our own cancellation quest . . . may our travels be long, may the wind be at our backs, and may we never run out of open roads to drive, nor days in which to drive them.

Introduction

Passport Stampers, Start Your Engines!

So you've crisscrossed the United States by car, plane, train, and bus, you've traversed scenic rivers by powerboat, airboat, kayak, and canoe, you've hiked rolling foothills, climbed summits, and gazed down into massive canyons. You've stood at the top of Yosemite National Park's Sentinel Dome, trekked across the fire-hot sands of Death Valley, canoed the rushing Middle Delaware River, and camped among the alligators in the Everglades. You've visited every major Civil War battlefield and every president's mansion, and you've seen every bed in which George Washington once slept.

That's all great, but did you get the Passport cancellation?

The coveted Passport cancellation—the symbol of the Passport To Your National Parks® program—has moved from its humble beginning as a souvenir of happy National Park travelers to become a goal in itself. Today more than 1.3 million families own the little blue book that has developed into a national pastime, and more than 75,000 of these books sell in National Park bookstores every year.

If you're a Passport owner, you know what I know: Passport cancellation collecting is no casual matter. Chances are you've planned at least one vacation with the goal of visiting the most national park sites in a single day or week, stopping at each visitor center to stamp your Passport book with the 1¼-inch-wide, dated cancellation that proves you were there.

The Passport To Your National Parks® is a breast-pocket-sized book that contains instructions for its use, basic maps of each of its nine regions, and blank pages for the collection of rubber stamp cancellations and for sets of colorful, adhesive-backed stamps issued on an annual basis. Collectors will stop at Passport cancellation stations in whatever national park they visit and imprint their Passport books with the rubber stamp cancellation they find there. Each cancellation has an adjustable date, so it is a permanent reminder of the very day the Passport holder visited the park.

Cancellations record the date of your visit.

While the National Park Service currently divides the nation into seven geographic regions, the Passport program recognizes nine regional divisions to achieve an even distribution of parks over all of the service's geographic regions. Regions are designated in the Passport book by color, and each region includes a color-block map of included states, a list of the parks in that region, and blank pages for collection of *two* kinds of stamps: the *rubber stamp cancellations* showcased in this guide and *full-color, self-adhesive stamps* that are part of the Passport To Your National Parks® Annual Stamp Series.

The color-coding extends to the cancellations themselves: Cancellation stamps at each national park have ink colors that coincide with their regional divisions. In other words, a cancellation in Pennsylvania will have light blue ink to match the Mid-Atlantic Region's designated color in the Passport book, a Maine cancellation will have golden brown ink to match the North Atlantic Region's color, and so on.

It may also be interesting to note that some cancellations are expressed through a combination of upper case and lower case type; others are typeset in all capital letters.

A note on the Annual Stamp Series: The self-adhesive sets, issued every spring, include ten full-color stamps. One park from each of the nine regions is showcased on a separate stamp with a photograph and brief description; each set also includes a larger National Stamp honoring a park that's celebrating a special anniversary or milestone in that year. Like the cancellations, the self-adhesive stamps each have a color bar that matches the region's color, making them very easy to place on the correct pages in the Passport book. The stamp sets—including those issued in previous years—are readily available at the parks and on the Internet at www.eparks.com. *Because the stamp sets are so easy to obtain, they are not the focus of this Passport program companion guide. Instead, I focus on the cancellations, which must be secured at the various sites themselves.*

In 2006, the twentieth anniversary of the Passport program was recognized with the introduction of the Passport To Your National Parks® Explorer, a deluxe Passport package that provides more detailed maps, more stamping pages, a ring binder that allows users to insert and remove pages, a water-resistant, zipper-closed outer cover, pockets for maps, brochures, and personal items, a pen, and a handy carrying strap. The Passport To Your National Parks® companion guides are the right size to slip into the Explorer's inside pocket.

You may choose to chase every Passport cancellation in every park or affiliate, including the many duplicate cancellations scattered through far-flung visitor centers and other cancellation stations, or you may prefer to collect just one cancellation from each park as you happen across it. You also may want to collect "bonus cancellations," unofficial cancellations of every shape, size, color, and form, found in hundreds of national parks as well as in incalculable numbers of unrelated sites in every state (more on these below).

So successful is this program that there are now more than 1,500 cancellations available in 391 national parks and in dozens of National Park Service affiliates! This guide will tell you exactly where to find them, extending the pleasure of your travel experiences by taking you into areas you might never discover on your own. You'll see more of each park, you'll gain a better understanding of why the U.S. Department of the Interior preserves these natural, historic, and cultural places, and you'll come home with a sense of accomplishment and a burning desire to hit the road again as soon as possible . . . because there are more cancellations out there, more places to see, and more two-lane blacktop roads to conquer.

A (Very) Brief History of Passport To Your National Parks®

In 1986, the National Park Service entered into a joint agreement with Eastern National, the organization that owns and manages the bookstores in most of the national parks east of the Mississippi River. The idea was simple: Create a program that provides visitors to the national parks with a free memento and invites them to increase the frequency and quantity of their national park visits by encouraging them to collect Passport cancellations.

The Passport To Your National Parks® program began with just one cancellation at each park, but as it grew, so did the number of cancellations offered at many of the larger parks. Over the course of years, parks began to order additional cancellations. Participation in the program has always been voluntary, but no park has rejected the program (with the exception of Hohokam Pima National Monument in Arizona, which is not open to the public). In fact, hundreds of sites have chosen to expand the potential for Passport stamping within their boundaries. The smallest parks may have just one cancellation on the property, but the more expansive parks—Great Smoky Mountains, Yellowstone, Grand Canyon, Acadia, Olympic, Everglades, Delaware Water Gap, and many others—offer anywhere from five to seventeen cancellations in bookstores, visitor centers, museums, train depots, ranger stations, lighthouses, and information kiosks, luring collectors to stray from the main paths and discover the hidden treasures beyond.

This guide will help you find the cancellations that you want to collect, while bringing others to your attention that you might never find on your own. Collect the ones that interest you, ignore the rest, and enjoy the Passport program in the way that suits your lifestyle, your budget, and your enthusiasm.

Duplicate Versus Unique: Which Cancellations You'll Find in the Parks

As of this writing, more than 1,500 official Passport To Your National Parks® cancellations are documented throughout the 391 National Park Service sites, affiliated areas, and heritage corridors.

Many parks place duplicate cancellations at visitor centers and other sites throughout their units, providing easy access for collectors who may only make one stop within the park. For example, Acadia National Park in Maine offers a generic cancellation at every visitor center throughout the park, for a total of six duplicates. Meanwhile, at the same park, there are twelve cancellations with location-specific text, providing collectors with unique cancellations for Blackwood Campground, Schoodic Peninsula, Isle au Haut, Seawall Campground, Islesford, Jordan Pond, and others.

A generic, duplicate cancellation and a unique, place-specific cancellation.

Some Passport stampers collect all the duplicates as well as the unique cancellations they find in their travels. The idea of collecting an imprint from every Passport cancellation in the country appeals to some hard-core stampers, and they will return to parks again and again when new cancellations are added, even if they are identical to the originals.

Other collectors will skip the duplicates, collecting only the unique cancellations they find in each park. Each method provides its own rewards: Duplicate cancellation collecting will fill a Passport book quickly with places and dates, while collecting only the unique cancellations may save time on the road that would otherwise be spent chasing down duplicates.

In each park's entry, I note the number of unique cancellations and the number of duplicates to help you determine what you'd like to collect in the time you have. Cancellations that exist in only one location, with no duplicates, are noted in this guide as "unique" with a special ❶ icon. These are the most precious cancellations to most Passport cancellation collectors, as each is available at only one place in the entire country. Knowing which cancellations are unique will help you plan your travels for maximum collecting. Those cancellations that can be collected in any number of locations are noted in this book as "duplicate" with a corresponding ❷ icon.

Bonus Cancellations

In addition to the official cancellations, many Passport stampers collect the irregular "bonus" cancellation stamps they come across in their travels.

Bonus cancellations can come in any shape, size, or form. Some parks have a series of bonus cancellations in animal shapes, while others provide a commemorative cancellation to celebrate an important anniversary or milestone. Some are complex, depicting an entire landscape, scene, or architectural detail, while still others are simply larger and square instead of the regulation size and circular shape.

Travelers find these additional cancellations within and beyond the perimeters of the national parks: in the bookstores or offices of state-owned parks and historic sites, at presidential libraries, or at privately owned attractions. The rampant success of the Passport program certainly would encourage sites that are not part of this or any other stamping program to join in the fun.

A complete list of these odd and often transitory bonus cancellations would make this book too unwieldy to carry on stamping trips, but if you would like a list of all the bonus cancellations documented to date, visit www.parkstamps.org (the National Park Travelers Club Web site) and click on Master List.

About Changed and Missing Cancellations and Where to Send Updates

The Passport To Your National Parks® companion series endeavors to bring you the most accurate information possible about where to find Passport cancellation stamps in all National Park Service sites and affiliates.

Because the Passport program includes so many participating sites, changes can take place in the program without the knowledge of The Globe Pequot Press or this author. Cancellations sometimes wear out, become too damaged to use, are misplaced, or disappear entirely in the hands of selfish souvenir hounds. In addition, the increase in volunteers at national park sites, caused in part by recent budget constraints, means that many frontline information desk and visitor center assistants are not familiar with the Passport program.

Cancellations are often reordered, and staff members do not always order identical cancellations to those that have been lost or damaged. You are virtually certain to encounter occasional variations in spelling, punctuation, use of contractions, and actual wording on cancellations when compared to the cancellations listed in these guides. The original cancellation may be long gone or forgotten. You may hope that it is lingering in a desk drawer, waiting for an intrepid collector to inquire about it . . . but in reality, the chances of this are slim.

If you find that the cancellation you've collected at any site is not the one you expected, please contact me at found stamp@minetor.com. I will make note of the change, post it on my official Web site at www.minetor.com/travelbooks, and pass the change on to the National Park Travelers Club for updating on the club's Master List. If you can e-mail a jpeg scan of your cancellation and include the exact location in which you found it, as well as your name, you will receive acknowledgement for your efforts on www.minetor.com/travelbooks.

Please do not harass rangers or any other park staff member or volunteer about missing cancellations. If you've inquired and the cancellation is not available, it's time to move on to your next stop, or to take some time to enjoy the park, visitor center, contact station, or historic site and its surroundings.

Needless to say, if you're traveling to a particularly out-of-the-way stamping location, call before you drive to be sure the cancellation is available.

Some Rules for Collecting Cancellations

The first and most important rule of Passport cancellation collecting is to enjoy the parks, whether you visit for an hour, a day, a week, or an entire season. We collect Passport cancellations because we love the parks in which they are found. Walk, bike, swim, paddle, explore, and learn as you travel.

Perhaps it's not necessary to say this, but Rule #2 is to show respect for the parks. The old adage, "Take nothing but pictures, leave nothing but footprints," holds true every day, and Passport stampers are leaders in demonstrating their commitment to park preservation. Leave artifacts or natural resources where you find them, pack out your own litter and that of others, and do no harm to the landscapes you came to admire.

About "Stamp and Run"

Here comes the collector, Passport book in hand, dashing to the cancellation station a few minutes before closing. He grabs the cancellation stamp, flips pages, bangs the stamp down onto the ink pad and smacks a quick imprint into his book... then rushes out again, with hardly a word of greeting to the staff member, ignoring the educational displays and the items for sale in the bookstore.

The dreaded "stamp and run" is the fastest way to meet the angry side of a park ranger—both because of the stamper's obvious disinterest in the park itself, and because the stamp-and-run perpetrator can appear indifferent, unfriendly, or downright rude. Passport cancellation seekers take heed: The ranger who is frustrated by your apparent lack of interest could be the same ranger who will come to your aid when you've strayed off the trail in the forest, or help you limp back to the visitor center when you turn an ankle on a rocky path.

If you must stamp and run, stop for a moment to explain the reasons for your abrupt behavior to the ranger or staffer behind the desk. Ask the ranger what's new at the park, and listen to the options for ways to extend your visit or plan a return trip. We all encounter days when nothing goes as planned, and we arrive at a park just in time to stamp the Passport before the visitor center shuts down for the night. But there still may be a pleasant twilight walk, an unexplored path, a previously overlooked historic structure, or a turnout with a wondrous view that we did not know existed until we asked.

Talk to Passport Fans Online

Thanks to the Web, Passport cancellation collectors from all over the country can connect and talk to one another, sharing lists of cancellations, secrets for obtaining record numbers of cancellations in single trips, and much, much more.

One of the best resources you'll find online is the Master List, a gargantuan Microsoft Excel document updated on a biweekly basis by Nancy Bandley. Known as the "Stamp Queen," Nancy boarded a seaplane with her husband, Dennis, and reached her 388th park—Aniakchak National Monument and Preserve in Alaska—in June 2005. This list not only catalogs all of the official cancellations, it also lists every bonus, or unofficial, cancellation discovered to date, as well as the lost, retired, or stolen cancellations that are no longer available.

You can find the list on a Web discussion board run by the National Park Travelers Club at www.parkstamps.org, one of several sites at which Passport cancellation collectors share anecdotes and discoveries from the road.

If a motorcycle is your preferred vehicle, check out the Iron Butt Association's National Park Service Motorcycle Touring forum at http://forums.delphiforums.com/NPSTouring/messages. These itinerant road warriors consider traveling from park to park an endurance sport. They know all the ins and outs of collecting, and their tips for safe, long-distance riding are invaluable to any cycle enthusiast.

How to Use This Book

This companion guide series is divided into nine books to match the regions in the Passport program. The states are listed alphabetically within each region, and the parks are alphabetized within each state.

In this volume, all stamping locations are in the eastern time zone.

In addition to the official 391 national parks, you'll find national park affiliated areas and National Heritage Areas and Corridors listed within each state. Virtually all of these affiliates have Passport cancellations, although participation in the Passport program is spottier because the sites are less centralized. Management of affiliated areas and National Heritage Areas and Corridors is in the hands of state and local agencies rather than the National Park Service. Some are exquisitely managed and maintained—the Oklahoma City National Memorial is a standout in this regard—while others are spread out across a wide geographic area, making it more difficult for management to keep tabs on the location and maintenance of Passport cancellations.

Here's what you'll find on each page of this guide:

- The official National Park Service name and designation for the park.

- The state and town or city in which the park is located (or where the park's headquarters is located for multilocation parks).

- The park's main information telephone number and Web address—you'll need these to double check park hours, to make certain that the park is actually open on the day you want to go there, and to plan the activities you'd like to enjoy during your visit. Even though park hours are provided in this book, anything from bad weather to budget shortages can close a visitor center or outlying building without notice.

- The park's time zone. In this guide, all parks are within the eastern time zone, so this entry has been omitted.
- Total number of cancellations at each park.
- The degree of difficulty in obtaining the park's Passport cancellations. Every park has a rating of **Easy, Tricky, Challenging,** or **Heroic,** helping you understand the hurdles you must vault to collect all of the cancellations in each park.

   Easy: The park is open 362 days or more each year and has only one or two cancellations, which are readily accessible at the bookstore or visitor center. Essentially, if you show up during business hours any day but Thanksgiving, Christmas, or New Year's Day, the cancellation is yours.

   Tricky: Something's up at this park, and you'll need to be alert to get the cancellation. The park is open only during limited hours or on an erratic or seasonal schedule. There's more than one cancellation, and there's an obstacle—the cancellation stamp is hidden in a desk drawer, a long-closed visitor center waiting for repairs, a task that must be performed before the cancellation can be obtained. Look for the "Stamping tips" to find out what's going on.

   Challenging: There are lots of cancellations in this park, and it may take more than one day to get them all and still enjoy what this park has to offer. Cancellation collecting may require an unusual physical effort, like a long walk (more than a mile) to the stamping site, or the many units involved are open on a limited basis. You'll go well out of your way to finish stamping in this park. The "Stamping tips" will help you figure out what to do—and for the parks with the most cancellations, there's a suggested route for maximum stamping success.

   Heroic: Slap on that seasickness patch and strap in! You'll need to endure a long ferry ride—or two—on choppy water, charter a seaplane, or jet out to an exotic island to get this one. There may be only one cancellation at each of these parks, but it will be hard-won, and you'll be talking about this trip for years to come.

- A short description of the park and why it exists, providing baseline information about what you can see, do, or learn when you go.
- "Stamping tips," with cautions, twists, and turns encountered by some of the most well traveled Passport participants in the country.
- "Don't miss this!" takes you beyond the brochure to find the gems in each park—sights, sounds, and activities you might not discover on your own. Don't miss this! is highlighted with an 🅘 icon.
- Park hours and fees are broken down by individual visitor center or other cancellation stamp location.
- Driving directions to the sites from the nearest major highways or cities.
- Stamping locations and what the cancellations say is the meat-and-potatoes for each park. The cancellation's specific location, any pertinent information on that location, and the cancellation's exact text is provided in this section. The text on each cancellation is listed uniformly to help you determine if you have found the correct cancellation. The text that arches around the top half of the cancellation is listed first. A "/" (forward slash) signals the end of the top text, and the text following the "/" fills the bottom half of the cancellation. The text is listed exactly as it appears on the cancellation: *If it's listed in this guide in all capital letters, then the cancellation itself was made that way. Occasionally a misspelling appears on a cancellation; these are not corrected in this guide, but presented as they appear.*

Unique cancellations are identified with a 🅤. These cancellations have no duplicates. There's only one place to find each of these, so you'll want to build stops for these cancellations into your travel plans.

Duplicated cancellations are identified with a 🅓. These cancellations can be found in more than one place.

While we believe that all the existing cancellations have been cataloged here, you may come across new or hitherto undetected official Passport cancellation stamps that are not in this book. If so, we want to hear from you! Please send any updates to me at foundstamp@minetor.com. Include the text of the cancellation, the place you found it, and as much detail as possible about where this cancellation resides. If possible, send a jpeg scan of the cancellation. I'll post updates at my Web site for this purpose, www.minetor.com/travelbooks.

In addition to this book and your official Passport, you need one more thing: America the Beautiful—The National Parks and Federal Recreational Lands Pass. This pass will provide you and the other passengers in your single-family vehicle (or your spouse, parents, and children) with free or discounted admission for one year to every park site in the system, as well as other sites managed by the federal government. You'll find that your pass will pay for itself in one trip. Purchase your pass from the National Parks Foundation at www.nationalparks.org, or at any national park site.

Buckle up—it's time to hit the road.

The National Capital Region

Oh, the joys of collecting Passport cancellations in Washington, D.C., where dozens exist within walking distance of one another! It's easy to rack up a lot of park visits in a short time here—in fact, a single stamping day might net you thirty cancellations or more if you begin at the three locations that offer eleven to nineteen cancellations each (see "Special Stamping Locations"). It's possible to collect all the cancellations and complete the entire National Capital Region in the space of a few days, if you're traveling in summer and your plans include weekdays—especially if you save the major memorials on the National Mall for the evening, when the historic sites have closed and you can enjoy the dramatic evening lighting that makes these monuments even larger than the larger-than-life people they honor.

With so much wonderful Passport stamping to do here, however, it's important to take time to appreciate the parks and monuments, to understand the meaning behind the many messages you'll read in granite and marble, and to feel the pulse of this remarkable city, where people of every race, party, philosophy, and skill level come together in the capital of the free world.

Washington, D.C., is the city of symbols, honoring the men and women who have become icons of our heritage—some whose destiny required greatness, and some who were ordinary people achieving extraordinary things. The wonder of Washington is in its ability to capture significant achievements at every level, from the emancipation of African American slaves to the labors of the Civilian Conservation Corps, and from the signing of a document that declared America free to the service and sacrifice of millions whose lives were lost over-seas. Here the Passport program takes you beyond the National Mall to the homes-turned-offices in which determined individuals created organizations with nationwide and even global reach, and to natural areas dragged back from the brink of ecological disaster by local and federal efforts. Washington has its well-known heroes, but your Passport will show you the lesser known as well, the people whose diligence, ingenuity, and commitment made the difference for millions.

As thorough as the Passport program has been in distribut-ing cancellations throughout the National Capital Region, new park properties emerge occasionally. Cancellations may not be ordered for these new parks, sites, or trails until the site is fully prepared to give visitors a quality park experience. As of this writing, the new Captain John Smith Chesapeake National His-toric Trail has no Passport cancellation stamps for this reason. In addition, Meridian Hill Park—listed on the National Park Service Web site as a separate park in Washington, D.C.—is actually managed by Rock Creek Park and does not have a cancellation stamp.

Just before this guide went to press, the Underground Net-work to Freedom added cancellations at sites in this region. While a dedicated entry is not provided, cancellations are listed in the guide.

A tip for your travels: Take the train, bus, and the Tourmo-bile. Leave your car outside the city—the mass transit system will serve you well, even in reaching sites well beyond the National Mall. Get the Metrobus and Metrorail schedules and routes at www.wmata.com. Once you're in town, the Tourmo-bile will take you to every major monument and to Arlington National Cemetery. A one-day pass allows you to board the shuttle from any point along its route, and to get on and off throughout the day as often as you like. Get the tour stop map at www.tourmobile.com, and order your tickets from Ticket-master at (800) 551–SEAT, or buy them as you board the shut-tle. The $20 daily price may seem high, but you'll wish you'd sprung for it by late morning as you walk the long stretches from one monument to the next.

Special Stamping Locations

Of the many things that are unique about stamping in the nation's capital, the most significant is that there are three offices in the Washington, D.C., area that hold eleven to nineteen Passport cancellations each! Stops at these offices net cancellations that can be found nowhere else in the region (such as those for some of the memorials on the National Mall), as well as duplicate cancellations for some of the out-of-the-way monuments, parkways, and smaller parks. I'm sharing these locations with you so that you can refer back to them as you study entries in this guide for national park sites: Whenever a duplicate or unique cancellation for the site can be found at one of these "stamp stash" locations, I've listed it with an asterisk (*) to let you know that many other cancellations are also available at this office.

These stamping nuclei offer opportunities to chat with particularly enthusiastic national park rangers who not only appreciate the value of the Passport To Your National Parks® program, but who love to meet collectors and talk about your travels in America. It may feel like cheating to stop and gather so many cancellations in just a few locations, but these stops are a special treat, an experience you won't find anywhere else in the national park system.

Here are the "secret" places with colossal cancellation stashes.

1 George Washington Memorial Parkway: Turkey Run Park Headquarters

McLean, Virginia
(703) 289–2500
www.nps.gov/gwmp

Number of cancellations: Sixteen, including twelve at parkway headquarters and four at the ranger station in Turkey Run Park

Difficulty: Tricky

About this site: See the listing for George Washington Memorial Parkway in the Virginia chapter in this guide.

Stamping tips: Note that the headquarters is open only on weekdays—be sure to make this a first stop if you're arriving on Friday for the weekend. As virtually all other sites in the National Capital Region keep weekend as well as weekday hours, you can still get the majority of these cancellations at their native sites if you can't reach this office during its business hours.

George Washington Memorial Parkway also has a ranger station in Turkey Run Park with four of the same cancellations. However, the rangers are often in the field, conducting educational programs or carrying out their duties, so this station will most likely be closed and locked during the park's busiest months (spring, summer, and fall), even though it is officially open. Don't despair! In acknowledgment of the Passport program's importance to its participants, Parkway rangers requested that duplicate cancellations be kept at the Arlington National Cemetery Bookstore, where they are available to collectors year-round on any day of the week.

Cancellations at the ranger station in Turkey Run Park—all of which are duplicated at the Arlington bookstore—are as follows:

☐ George Washington Memorial Parkway/McLean, VA Ⓓ

☐ Lyndon B Johnson Memorial Grove/Washington D.C. Ⓓ

☐ Theodore Roosevelt Island/Washington, D.C. Ⓓ

☐ Marine Corps Memorial / Netherlands Carillon/Arlington, VA Ⓓ

Hours: Open Monday–Friday, 7:45 A.M.–4:15 P.M. Closed on all federal holidays.

Fees: Admission to Turkey Run Park is free.

How to get there: Turkey Run Park is located in McLean, Virginia, 2 miles off the Capital Beltway (Interstate 495) on the George Washington Memorial Parkway (GWMP).

From beltway exit 43 (old exit 14), follow the GWMP 2 miles to the Turkey Run Park exit on the right. Follow signs into the park.

From Washington, D.C., and Old Town Alexandria, take the GWMP north approximately 8 miles and exit right at the Turkey Run Park sign. Make the first right turn into the park.

Stamping Locations and What the Cancellations Say

Turkey Run Park Headquarters

- ☐ Arlington House, Robert E. Lee Memorial/Arlington, VA ⓓ
- ☐ Clara Barton National Historic Site/Glen Echo, MD ⓓ
- ☐ CLARA BARTON PARKWAY/MD GWMP VA ⓓ
- ☐ George Washington Memorial Parkway/McLean, VA ⓓ
- ☐ Glen Echo Park/Glen Echo, MD ⓓ
- ☐ Great Falls Park/Great Falls, VA ⓓ
- ☐ Lyndon B Johnson Memorial Grove/Washington D.C. ⓓ
- ☐ Potomac Heritage/National Scenic Trail ⓓ
- ☐ Theodore Roosevelt Island/Washington, D.C. ⓓ
- ☐ Marine Corps Memorial / Netherlands Carillon/Arlington, VA ⓓ
- ☐ Women In Military Service for America Memorial/Arlington, VA ⓓ
- ☐ GW Mem. Pkwy. HQ./Underground RR Freedom Network ⓤ

2 National Capital Parks–East Headquarters

Washington, D.C.
(202) 690–5185
www.nps.gov/nace

Number of cancellations: Thirteen

Difficulty: Tricky

About this site: The management umbrella for fourteen major park areas in Washington, D.C., National Capital Parks–East provides oversight for the following national park sites: Anacostia Park (including Kenilworth Park and Aquatic Gardens), some of the Fort Circle Parks that form the Civil War Defenses of Washington (Fort Dupont, Fort Foote, and Fort Washington), Frederick

Douglass National Historic Site, Harmony Hall, Mary McLeod Bethune Council House National Historic Site, Capitol Hill Parks, Greenbelt Park, Oxon Cove Park/Oxon Hill Farm, Piscataway Park (including the National Colonial Farm), Sewall–Belmont House National Historic Site, Baltimore–Washington Parkway, and Suitland Parkway.

Stamping tips: When this guide went to press, the headquarters office was in Anacostia Park. Legislation passed in 2007 required that the office be moved to a new location; call before visiting to confirm the office address.

Like most offices in the National Capital Region, this one is only open on weekdays during regular business hours. If you're coming to Washington for the weekend, make this one of your first stops on Friday. Nine of the cancellations found here are unique and not available anywhere else. Be sure to collect them here (they're noted below).

Hours: Open Monday–Friday, 8:30 A.M.–4:00 P.M. Closed Thanksgiving, Christmas, and New Year's Day.

Fees: There is no admission fee for this office.

How to get there: To reach Anacostia Park from the Baltimore–Washington Parkway/MD 295, travel south toward Washington, D.C., When the parkway intersects MD 295, follow the lanes left toward Interstate 495/Capital Beltway. Take the eastbound Pennsylvania Avenue exit. Take the first right onto Fairlawn Avenue. Go to the stop sign and turn right again on Nicholson Street to enter the park.

From Interstate 395, travel north into Washington, D.C., toward the Southeast/Southwest Freeway. When the freeway splits, veer right toward Martin Luther King, Jr. Avenue, then take the Anacostia Park exit to the stop sign. Turn right onto Good Hope Road to enter the park.

From Suitland Parkway/South Capitol Street, go west toward Washington, D.C., Turn right at the traffic signal onto Firth Sterling Avenue. Take a left at the next traffic signal onto Howard Road. When you approach the Douglass Bridge, the lanes will split and the park entrance is to the right.

Stamping Locations and What the Cancellations Say

☐ ANACOSTIA PARK/WASHINGTON, D.C. **❶**

☐ Baltimore–Washington Pkwy/Greenbelt, MD **❶**

- ☐ CAPITOL HILL PARKS/WASHINGTON, D.C. **①**
- ☐ FORT CIRCLE PARKS/WASHINGTON, D.C. **①**
- ☐ FORT DUPONT PARK/WASHINGTON, D.C. **❶**
- ☐ FREDERICK DOUGLASS NHS/WASHINGTON, D.C. **❶**
- ☐ Greenbelt Park/Greenbelt, MD **①**
- ☐ HARMONY HALL/FORT WASHINGTON, MD. **①**
- ☐ KENILWORTH PARK AND/AQUATIC GARDENS **①**
- ☐ MARY McLEOD BETHUNE COUNCIL HOUSE NHS/
  WASHINGTON, D.C. **❶**
  (oversized cancellation)
- ☐ NATIONAL CAPITAL PARKS–EAST/WASHINGTON, D.C. **①**
  (two identical cancellations are available)
- ☐ SEWALL–BELMONT HOUSE/WASHINGTON, D.C. **❶**
- ☐ SUITLAND PARKWAY/WASH, DC/SUITLAND, MD **①**

3 Survey Lodge on the National Mall

Washington, D.C.
(202) 426–6841
www.nps.gov/mall
Number of cancellations: Nineteen
Difficulty: Easy
About this site: This is the ranger station for all of the parks on the National Mall, and as such it serves as a clearinghouse for information on everything from Constitution Gardens to the World War II Memorial. You'll find cancellations here for the memorials that are affiliated with the national parks but are not official park sites in themselves, as well as duplicates for many of the most well-known and popular memorials.

Don't miss this! You've collected the cancellations here for several memorials that you can't obtain anywhere else. Good for you! Now, make a point of picking up a map, asking a ranger to point out where the memorials are, and walking across the National Mall to take a look at them. Each recognizes a significant individual or group with whom you may or may not be familiar, and it will take only a few minutes to appreciate the contributions these people made to our nation's development. These memorials are all described later in this book.

Hours: Open 8:30 A.M.–7:00 P.M. daily (hours are approximate and may change slightly with seasons). Closed Christmas.

Fees: There is no admission fee for this office.

How to get there: Interstates 66 and 395 provide access to the Mall from the south. Interstate 495, New York Avenue, Rock Creek Parkway, George Washington Memorial Parkway, and the Cabin John Parkway provide access from the north. I-66, U.S. Highway 50, and U.S. Highway 29 provide access from the west. Route 50, U.S. Highway 1, and Maryland 4 provide access from the east. The Survey Lodge is in the southwest section of the Washington Monument's grounds.

Stamping Locations and What the Cancellations Say

☐ Constitution Gardens/Washington, D.C. ⓓ

☐ District of Columbia World War Memorial/Washington, D.C. ⓤ

☐ FRANKLIN DELANO ROOSEVELT MEMORIAL/ WASHINGTON, D.C. ⓓ

☐ George Mason Memorial/Washington, D.C. ⓤ

☐ John Ericsson Memorial/Washington, D.C. ⓤ

☐ John Paul Jones Memorial/Washington, D.C. ⓤ

☐ Korean War Veterans Memorial/Washington D.C. ⓓ

☐ Lincoln Memorial/Washington D.C. ⓓ

☐ MEM to the 56 Signers of the Dec. of Independence/ Washington, D.C. ⓤ

☐ National Capital Region/Washington, D.C. ⓓ

☐ National Mall/Washington, DC ⓓ

☐ National Mall and Memorial Parks/Washington D.C. ⓓ

☐ Pennsylvania Avenue Nat'l Historic Site/Washington, D.C. ⓓ

☐ Ulysses S. Grant Memorial/Washington, D.C. ⓤ

☐ Thomas Jefferson Memorial/Washington, D.C. ⓓ

☐ Vietnam Veterans Memorial/Washington, DC ⓓ

☐ Washington Monument/Washington, D.C. ⓓ

☐ West Potomac Park/Washington, DC ⓤ

☐ World War II Memorial/Washington, D.C. ⓓ

Maryland

4 Baltimore–Washington Parkway

Part of National Capital Parks–East
Greenbelt, Maryland
(301) 344–3948
www.nps.gov/bawa

Number of cancellations: Five: three for the parkway, plus two for Greenbelt Park

Difficulty: Tricky

About this site: A scenic highway connecting Washington, D.C., with Baltimore, Maryland, this 29-mile stretch of roadway actually was conceived by Pierre L'Enfant, a captain in the U.S. Engineers (predecessor of the U.S. Army Corps of Engineers) who was commissioned by President George Washington to draw up an architectural plan for the United States federal capital. The parkway concept did not receive government approval until 1902—and then only for bicycle and horse-drawn carriage traffic—and more than fifty years passed before the road opened to auto traffic in 1954. No trucks or other commercial vehicles may use this scenic road.

Stamping tips: If you want all three variations of this cancellation, you'll need to visit on a weekday. The Greenbelt Park Ranger Station is open seven days a week, but the National Capital Parks–East headquarters keeps weekday business hours.

Don't miss this! Before you reach Washington, there's a treasure trove of places to stop along this fairly short road, from nature centers to military installations. Fort Meade, one of the main training centers for troops from World War I through Operation Desert Shield, houses the first U.S. Army Museum, a showplace for exhibition of military artifacts. The NASA Goddard Space Flight Center welcomes visitors to its interactive Earth Gallery, where you have the opportunity to learn about scientists' most current understanding of our planet's natural systems. For the energetic, a two-and-a-half-hour walking tour provides a complete overview of Goddard's role in the national space program since its inception. The National Arboretum brims with visual interest at any time of the year, with display gardens filled with azaleas, holly, magnolias, and many other perennials, all nestled within eastern deciduous forests. You can also take a tram tour of the Patuxent National Wildlife Refuge, a combined recreational and research area where any hike or tour will provide views of resident wildlife.

Hours: The parkway is open twenty-four hours a day, seven days a week, year-round. Greenbelt Park headquarters is open Monday to Friday, 8:00 A.M. to 4:00 P.M.

Greenbelt Park Ranger Station is open daily from 8:00 A.M. to 3:45 P.M. For details on National Capital Parks–East, see its listing in this guide.

Fees: There are no fees for use of the parkway.

How to get there: To travel the parkway, start at Baltimore's Inner Harbor and drive west on Lombard Street. Turn left on Green Street and follow it to Russell Street. Continue south on Russell Street. This street becomes the Baltimore–Washington Parkway (Maryland 295) when it leaves the city. Continue southwest on MD 295 through a small portion of Baltimore County, into the northeastern edge of Anne Arundel County, and, finally, through Prince George's County. Exit the parkway at U.S. Highway 50 west. Once across the Anacostia River, you are in the District of Columbia. Continue west. The byway ends when the road becomes New York Avenue.

To reach the cancellations at Greenbelt Park, take the Baltimore–Washington Parkway north to Maryland 193/Greenbelt Road West. Continue to the second traffic light. The park is on the left across from T.G.I. Friday's restaurant and the Marriott Courtyard.

Stamping Locations and What the Cancellations Say
Greenbelt Park Headquarters

☐ BALTIMORE–WASHINGTON PARKWAY/GREENBELT, MD **Ⓤ**
☐ GREENBELT PARK/GREENBELT, MD **Ⓓ**

Ranger station at Greenbelt Park campground

☐ BALTIMORE WASHINGTON PARKWAY/GREENBELT MD ⓤ

☐ GREENBELT PARK/GREENBELT, MD ⓓ

National Capital Parks–East headquarters*

☐ Baltimore–Washington Pkwy/Greenbelt, MD ⓤ

5 Clara Barton National Historic Site

Glen Echo, Maryland
(301) 492–6245
www.nps.gov/clba

Number of cancellations: Three: two unique (one all caps and one upper- and lowercase) for Clara Barton National Historic Site, plus one for Clara Barton Parkway

Difficulty: Easy

About this site: If you haven't heard of Clara Barton, ask any seven-year-old girl: The founder of the American Red Cross stands as one of the greatest female role models in American history. In her Washington, D.C., home (not this house), Barton established the organization that would grow to provide medical assistance, emergency care, aid to prisoners, solace, and help to victims of war and natural disasters in every community in the country, and to war-torn regions around the world. Beginning with the help she offered Civil War soldiers holed up in the U.S. Capitol building in 1861, Barton turned her downtown home into a clearinghouse for the receipt, storage, and distribution of medical supplies. A year later, she gained permission to transport supplies to battlefields, and her legendary ministrations to wounded soldiers turned her into a national icon. She moved thirty wagonloads of supplies to the house in Glen Echo in 1892, and then moved here herself in 1897, remodeling the house to serve as a residence and national Red Cross headquarters.

ⓘ **Don't miss this!** You don't need to take the tour to get the cancellation, but take it anyway. You're not here to see riches and fine interior decoration, but to see what one woman accomplished through her own initiative. Frills and finery were of no interest to Clara Barton, a woman who devoted her life to a career in leadership long before women were "allowed" to do such a thing.

The National Park Service restored eleven rooms of this house, focusing on the offices and the way the vast American Red Cross organization conducted business here. If you can't imagine how you could live and work without e-mail, word processing, and electronic spreadsheets, think how much Barton and her staff accomplished with just a few typewriters, paper, and pens. With these tools, the Red Cross orchestrated the organization of aid efforts for victims of disasters including hurricanes in South Carolina, the devastating Johnstown flood, the attack on the USS *Maine,* the Spanish-American War, tidal wave victims in Texas, typhoid and yellow fever epidemics, and countless others.

Hours: The Clara Barton National Historic Site is open daily from 10:00 A.M. to 5:00 P.M. The house is shown by guided tour only; tours start on the hour, with the first at 10:00 A.M. and last at 4:00 P.M. It is closed on Thanksgiving, Christmas, and New Year's Day.

George Washington Memorial Parkway: Turkey Run Park Headquarters is open Monday through Friday from 7:45 a.m. to 4:15 p.m. It is closed on all federal holidays.

Fees: Admission to this park is free.

How to get there: From Virginia, follow Interstate 495 west and north toward Rockville, Maryland. Cross the Potomac River on the American Legion Bridge, and take exit 41, which is immediately at the Maryland end of the bridge. Follow the signs reading CLARA BARTON PARKWAY–EAST, GLEN ECHO AND CLARA BARTON NATIONAL HISTORIC SITE, bearing right. Follow the Clara Barton Parkway approximately 2.25 miles and take the left ramp to MacArthur Boulevard. Turn left at the three-way stop sign and follow the signs to Clara Barton National Historic Site.

From Maryland, follow I–495 west and south toward northern Virginia. Take exit 40, Cabin John Parkway. The Cabin John Parkway merges with the Clara Barton Parkway. Follow the directions above once you reach the Clara Barton Parkway.

From Washington, D.C./Georgetown, use Canal Road to reach the Clara Barton Parkway; follow the directions above from Clara Barton Parkway.

Stamping Locations and What the Cancellations Say

Visitor center at house

☐ CLARA BARTON NATIONAL HISTORIC SITE/GLEN ECHO, MD ⓤ

☐ CLARA BARTON PARKWAY/MD GWMP VA ⓓ

George Washington Memorial Parkway: Turkey Run Park Headquarters*

☐ Clara Barton National Historic Site/Glen Echo, MD ⓤ

6 Clara Barton Parkway

Part of George Washington Memorial Parkway
Greenbelt, Maryland
(301) 492–6245
www.nps.gov/clba (this park has no office or Web site of its own)

Number of cancellations: Five: two for the parkway in Maryland, one more in Washington, D.C. In addition you'll find a cancellation for Glen Echo Park and one for Clara Barton National Historic Site at sites that have parkway cancellations.

Difficulty: Easy

About this site: In 1989, President George H. W. Bush renamed a portion of the George Washington Parkway in Maryland and Washington, D.C., for the nurse and humanitarian who founded the American Red Cross. This honor, while well deserved, stemmed from a practical decision to differentiate this road from the rest of the George Washington Parkway across the Potomac in Virginia. The Clara Barton Parkway runs along the Maryland shore of the Potomac River between the capital city and the Capital Beltway/Interstate 495.

Stamping tips: A word to the wise: If you're thinking of driving the length of the parkway to actualize your cancellations, veteran collector and Clara Barton Parkway volunteer Dan Elias notes that this road is primarily used as a commuter route to Washington, D.C. This means that sections of the parkway are one-way only during rush hours: inbound to Washington, D.C., in the morning, and outbound to Maryland in the afternoon. Be sure to take this into consideration when you plan your scenic drive.

🛈 **Don't miss this!** Much of the parkway runs parallel to the C&O Canal Towpath, providing especially pleasant opportunities for biking the length of this scenic road on groomed or paved paths. Volunteer Dan Elias and Susan Finta, a Clara Barton Parkway staff member, recommend an excursion to the Carderock picnic area on the C&O Canal because of its proximity to two particularly nice trails: Billy Goat "B" and "C" sections. According to Elias, the Billy Goat trails are well marked, skirting along the Potomac River and occasionally requiring scrambling over rocks. They are fun routes that provide scenic views of the river and usually are not as crowded as trails closer to Great Falls Tavern Visitor Center. For more information on the Billy Goat trails, download the map at www.nps.gov/choh/Recreation/Trails/greatfallstrailmap.pdf.

Hours: The Clara Barton Parkway is open twenty-four hours a day, seven days a week, year-round.

The Clara Barton National Historic Site is open daily from 10:00 A.M. to 5:00 P.M. The house is shown by guided tour only; tours start on the hour, with the first at 10:00 A.M. and last at 4:00 P.M. It is closed on Thanksgiving, Christmas, and New Year's Day.

The Glen Echo Park Visitor Center is open daily from 9:00 A.M. to 6:00 P.M. and closed Thanksgiving and Christmas.

Fees: There is no fee for use of the parkway. Admission to Clara Barton National Historic Site and Glen Echo Park is free.

How to get there: From Virginia take I–495 north toward Maryland. As soon as you cross the Potomac River, take exit 41 and keep bearing to the right as you exit. The first of six parking areas is located at the bottom of the ramp on the other side of the parkway.

From Maryland, take I–495 south toward Virginia. Use exit 40 to the Cabin John Parkway. After a mile or so, this becomes the Clara Barton Parkway. The first of four parking areas is located on the right soon after joining the Clara Barton Parkway.

Stamping Locations and What the Cancellations Say

Clara Barton National Historic Site
Located inside house
- ☐ CLARA BARTON PARKWAY/MD GWMP VA Ⓓ
- ☐ CLARA BARTON NATIONAL HISTORIC SITE/GLEN ECHO, MD Ⓤ

Glen Echo Park Visitor Center
Located in the lobby of the arcade building
- ☐ CLARA BARTON PARKWAY/MD GWMP VA Ⓓ
- ☐ Glen Echo Park/Glen Echo, MD Ⓓ

George Washington Memorial Parkway: Turkey Run Park Headquarters*
- ☐ CLARA BARTON PARKWAY/MD GWMP VA Ⓓ

7 Fort Foote Park

Part of National Capital Parks–East
Fort Washington, Maryland
(301) 763–4600
www.nps.gov/fofo

Number of cancellations: Seven: two for Fort Foote, plus two for Fort Washington, and one each for Piscataway Park, Harmony Hall, and Potomac Heritage National Scenic Trail

Difficulty: Easy

About this site: Named for Rear Admiral Andrew H. Foote (who died in combat in 1863, the year construction began here) and designed to replace the aging Fort Washington as a primary defense for the nation's capital, Fort Foote's impenetrable oval earthworks represented the finest military engineering of its day. The fort protected the river entrance to Alexandria and George-town, training two 15-inch Rodman guns and four Parrott rifles down the Potomac to stop enemies before they could come within 3 miles of the fort. Fort Foote is the southernmost fortifica-tion in the Defense of Washington Circle forts.

Stamping tips: The cancellations for this park actually live at Fort Washington. Note that if the visitor center is closed, one set of unique cancellations are kept in a box attached to the wall on the front porch of the fort.

❗ Don't miss this! The Rodman guns remain in place to this day, although the fort has not been used since World War I. Be sure to take a look at these remarkable cannons, as they represent some of the most powerful weaponry of the Civil War era.

Hours: Fort Foote is open daily from 9:00 A.M. to sunset. It is closed New Year's Day, Thanksgiving, and Christmas.

Fort Washington is open daily from April 1 through September 30 from 9:00 A.M. to 5:00 P.M. From October 1 to March 31, the fort is open from 9:00 A.M. to 4:30 P.M. It is closed Thanksgiving, Christmas, and New Year's Day.

Fees: Admission to this park is free.

How to get there: From the Capital Beltway (Interstate 95), take exit 3A, Indian Head Highway/Maryland 210, and drive south for about 3.5 miles to Old Fort Road. Turn right and proceed for one mile to Fort Foote Road South, then turn left. Follow the winding road through the residential area to the entrance on the left for the fort.

Stamping Locations and What the Cancellations Say

On the front porch of Fort Washington Visitor Center

Located in a box on the porch *only* when the visitor center is closed during regular business hours

☐ Fort Foote Park/Oxon Hill, MD **Ⓓ**

☐ Fort Washington Park/Fort Washington, MD **Ⓓ**

Inside Fort Washington Visitor Center

☐ Fort Foote Park/Oxon Hill, MD **Ⓤ**

☐ Fort Washington Park/Fort Washington, MD **Ⓓ**

☐ Piscataway Park/Accokeek, MD **Ⓤ**

☐ POTOMAC HERITAGE/NATIONAL SCENIC TRAIL **Ⓓ**

☐ Harmony Hall/Fort Washington, MD **Ⓤ**

8 Fort Washington Park

Part of National Capital Parks–East
Fort Washington, Maryland
(301) 763–4600
www.nps.gov/fowa

Number of cancellations: Seven: two for Fort Washington, and cancellations for Fort Foote, Harmony Hall, Piscataway Park, and Potomac Heritage National Scenic Trail

Difficulty: Easy

About this site: The only permanent fortification defending the city of Washington, D.C., until the Civil War, Fort Washington guarded the nation's capital from 1809 to 1921. The masonry fort we see today was built between 1814 and 1824. With changes in military technologies, masonry forts were replaced by structures of concrete and steel. Eight Endicott batteries constructed here as part of the Coastal Defense of the Potomac remained through World War I. The Third Battalion, Twelfth Infantry, the ceremonial unit of the Military District of Washington, called the grounds home until 1939.

Stamping tips: The management of this park has made it very easy to get the cancellation, even if the visitor center is closed when you arrive. The box on the front porch of the visitor center has a duplicate cancellation, so if you're not collecting an imprint from every cancellation that exists, you'll have no trouble adding Fort Washington to your "done" list.

Don't miss this! Most of the picnic areas around this fort are available by reservation only, so if you've taken the thirty-minute tour of the fort and you've walked the short foot trail along the Potomac…there's a lot more to see in the National Capital region.

Hours: The buildings are open daily from April 1 to September 30 from 9:00 A.M. to 5:00 P.M. From October 1 to March 31, the park is open from 9:00 A.M. to 4:30 P.M. It is closed Thanksgiving, Christmas, and New Year's Day. The grounds are open from 8:30 A.M. to sunset daily.

Fees: $3.00 per individual on foot or bicycle, good for three days; $5.00 per personal vehicle (car), good for three days

How to get there: From Washington, D.C., take the Capital Beltway (Interstate 495) to exit 3 (Indian Head Highway south/

Maryland 210 south). Keep left at the fork (Indian Head Highway south). Turn right on Fort Washington Road (less than 4 miles), continue through the traffic circle, keep right, and follow the road to the park entrance.

Stamping Locations and What the Cancellations Say
Inside Fort Washington Visitor Center

☐ Fort Washington Park/Fort Washington, MD Ⓓ
☐ Piscataway Park/Accokeek, MD Ⓤ
☐ POTOMAC HERITAGE/NATIONAL SCENIC TRAIL Ⓓ
☐ Fort Foote Park/Oxon Hill, MD Ⓤ
☐ Harmony Hall/Fort Washington, MD Ⓤ

On the front porch of Fort Washington
Located in a box when the visitor center is closed during regular business hours

☐ Fort Washington Park/Fort Washington, MD Ⓓ
☐ Fort Foote Park/Oxon Hill, MD Ⓓ

9 Glen Echo Park

Part of George Washington Memorial Parkway
Glen Echo, Maryland
(301) 492–6229
www.nps.gov/glec

Number of cancellations: Two

Difficulty: Easy

About this site: Taking its operating philosophy from the highly successful Chautauqua Institution in upstate New York, Glen Echo Park opened in 1871 as a center for the development of the mind and soul through participation in the sciences, language, arts, and literature. For nearly one hundred years, this meeting place for people seeking knowledge and enlightenment offered educational programs as well as cultural entertainment in the forms of music, dance, theater, and guest lectures. The park expanded its offerings in the early twentieth century to include a carousel, bumper car pavilion, and other amusement park attractions.

Today, all that remains of the original Tower of Philosophy is a small stone archway, but the carousel and bumper cars have been restored, and Glen Echo has regained its Chautauquan approach with a year-round concert series, lectures, and classes.

Don't miss this! Most collectors maintain a breakneck pace as they tour the National Capital Region because of the sheer number of cancellations available in close proximity. Consider slowing it down a bit for a couple of hours at Glen Echo, where you can take an art class (pottery, painting, photography, or glass art are all popular), enjoy a theater performance, or even learn some ballroom or contra dance steps. Glen Echo offers plenty of children's programs, so the whole family can find something new and different to do here. A full schedule of classes and events is available at www.glenechopark.org. At the very least, if you visit during the spring or summer, take a ride on the historic carousel with your family.

Hours: Open daily from 9:00 A.M. to 6:00 P.M. Closed Thanksgiving and Christmas.

Fees: Admission to the park is free. Some activities, including the carousel, have fees for admission.

How to get there: From Maryland, take the Capital Beltway (Interstate 495) to exit 40 (Cabin John/Clara Barton Parkways). From Virginia, take the Capital Beltway (I–495) to exit 41 east (Clara Barton/Cabin John Parkways, toward Washington). In both cases, stay in the leftmost lane of the parkway and travel 2.5 miles. Take the MacArthur Boulevard/Glen Echo exit from the parkway (the left exit). Travel slowly on the exit and follow the sign to MacArthur Boulevard, then turn left onto MacArthur. Go two blocks to Oxford Road (just beyond the Glen Echo shopping center) and turn left into the Glen Echo Park parking lot.

Stamping Locations and What the Cancellations Say

Visitor center
Located in the lobby of the arcade building
☐ Glen Echo Park/Glen Echo, MD ⓓ

George Washington Memorial Parkway: Turkey Run Park Headquarters*
☐ Glen Echo Park/Glen Echo, MD ⓓ

🔟 Greenbelt Park

Greenbelt, Maryland
(301) 344–3944
www.nps.gov/gree

Number of cancellations: Five: three for Greenbelt Park, plus two for Baltimore–Washington Parkway

Difficulty: Easy

About this site: There's no great geologic formation here, and no major event made history on this ground. What's remarkable about Greenbelt Park is that it exists at all in urban Washington, and that it contains the largest stand of forest inside the Beltway. Nine miles of hiking trails provide respite from city life, offering easy walks through Virginia pine and oak with bright red holly berries or edible blueberries poking through the understory.

❶ Don't miss this! Birders rejoice! Spring in Greenbelt Park is a treat for the eyes and ears, with nesting populations of many favorite songbird and migratory species, including eastern wood-pewee, Acadian flycatcher, red-eyed vireo, blue-gray gnatcatcher, wood thrush, pine warbler, ovenbird, scarlet tanager, and eastern towhee, to name just a few. Warblers abound, with hooded and Kentucky among the specialties. Even better, those pesky urban birds like rock pigeon, house sparrow, European starling, and house finch are rare in this park. Walk the Perimeter, Azalea, Dogwood, or Blueberry Trails to find nesting and migrating species.

Hours: Park headquarters are open from 8:00 A.M. to 4:00 P.M., Monday to Friday. The park ranger station (near the campground) is open from 8:00 A.M. to 3:45 P.M. seven days a week.

Fees: Admission to this park is free.

How to get there: From Interstate 95, take exit 23 onto Kenilworth Avenue/Maryland 201 and go south to Maryland 193/Greenbelt Road East. The park is a quarter-mile distant on the right; the address is 6565 Greenbelt Road (MD 193). From Washington, D.C., take the Baltimore–Washington Parkway (Interstate 295) north to Greenbelt Road West (MD 193). Proceed to the second traffic light. The park is on the left across from T.G.I. Friday's restaurant and the Marriott Courtyard.

Stamping Locations and What the Cancellations Say

Greenbelt Park Headquarters

☐ GREENBELT PARK/GREENBELT, MD **Ⓓ**
☐ BALTIMORE–WASHINGTON PARKWAY/GREENBELT, MD **Ⓤ**

Ranger station inside park

☐ GREENBELT PARK/GREENBELT, MD **Ⓓ**
☐ BALTIMORE WASHINGTON PARKWAY/GREENBELT MD **Ⓤ**
(This cancellation doesn't have the hyphen after Baltimore or the comma after Greenbelt, making it different from the cancellation at Greenbelt Park headquarters.)

National Capital Parks–East headquarters*

☐ Greenbelt Park/Greenbelt, MD **Ⓤ**

11 Oxon Cove Park/Oxon Hill Farm

Part of National Capital Parks–East
Oxon Hill, Maryland
(301) 839–1176
www.nps/gov/oxhi

Number of cancellations: Two, including one for the Underground Railroad

Difficulty: Easy

About this site: A working farm just off the Capital Beltway? It's true—Oxon Hill Farm served as a therapeutic and practical resource for the patients of Saint Elizabeths Hospital from the 1890s until the 1950s, providing fresh food for their consumption. Today the farm continues as a demonstration center, where visitors can observe just about every aspect of agricultural life much as it was in the late nineteenth century.

❗ Don't miss this! Make an advance reservation and try your own hand at milking a cow, gathering eggs from laying hens, or working the soil in the garden. You'll have the expert supervision of a ranger, and it's your option whether to jump in and participate or simply observe. But either way, you'll have the opportunity to get up close and personal with all the traditional barnyard animals—cattle, chickens, goats, sheep, rabbits, ducks, pigs, and a donkey. Before you visit, check the in-depth web site at www.nps.gov/nace/oxhi/visit.htm to see which seasonal activities may be available—sheepshearing, maple sugaring, plowing fields the old-fashioned way with horses and discs, crop harvesting, apple cider pressing, and more.

Hours: Open daily from 8:00 A.M. to 4:30 P.M. Closed Thanksgiving, Christmas, and New Year's Day.

Fees: Admission to this park is free.

How to get there: From downtown Washington, D.C., take Interstate 295 south (Kenilworth Avenue) to the Capital Beltway (Interstates 95/495). Take exit 1A, north toward Baltimore. On I–95/495, take exit 3A and bear right on the exit ramp onto Oxon Hill Road. Follow signs to the farm (a quick right turn).

From southeast Washington, D.C., take South Capitol Street, which becomes Indian Head Highway (Maryland 210); turn right onto Oxon Hill Road just beyond the Beltway. Follow signs to the farm.

From Alexandria, Virginia, take I–95/495 across the Potomac River (Woodrow Wilson Memorial Bridge). Remain on I–95/495 to the top of the hill. Take exit 3A and bear right on the exit ramp onto Oxon Hill Road. Follow signs to the farm (a quick right turn).

Stamping Locations and What the Cancellations Say

Oxon Cove Park Visitor Barn

- ☐ Oxon Cove Park/Oxon Hill, MD Ⓤ
- ☐ Oxon Cove Park/Underground RR Freedom Network Ⓤ

12 Piscataway Park

Accokeek, Maryland
(301) 763–4600
www.nps.gov/pisc

Number of cancellations: Two

Difficulty: Easy to get one stamp, tricky to get both

About this site: This is not so much a park as it is an environmental experiment. In an effort to preserve the view of the Potomac River as it was in George Washington's day, when he lived across the river at Mount Vernon, a pilot project was launched in 1952 employing conservation easements to prohibit urban expansion into a natural area. With so much effort invested in preserving this view, it's virtually required that we enjoy it—so this is a nice place for a picnic, a little bird-watching, or a tour of the National Colonial Farm, an outdoor living history museum that provides a view of middle-class tobacco farming in the eighteenth century.

Don't miss this! If you'd like to know how "regular people" lived the agricultural life in the late eighteenth century, the National Colonial Farm provides a refreshing perspective. Interpreters in period costume lead tours of the farm's tobacco barn, farmhouse, smokehouse, and residential outbuildings, while correct-to-period crops grow in a spacious garden. In addition to its usefulness as a museum, the farm also serves as a leader in historic plant preservation—so you'll see Orinoco tobacco and Virginia gourd-seed corn, crops that have become uncommon in our century.

Hours: The park is open daily during daylight hours.

The National Colonial Farm is open Tuesday to Sunday from 10:00 A.M. to 4:00 P.M. Winter hours may vary.

Fees: Admission to Piscataway Park is free. Admission to the National Colonial Farm is $2.00 for adults, 50 cents per child, and $5.00 per family

How to get there: Take exit 3A from the Capital Beltway (Interstate 95) to Maryland 210–S (Indian Head Highway), then go 10 miles to the intersection in Accokeek. Turn right onto Livingston

Road, then right onto Biddle Road. At the stop sign, turn right onto Bryan's Point Road and go 4 miles to the Potomac River.

Stamping Locations and What the Cancellations Say

Inside Fort Washington Visitor Center

☐ Piscataway Park/Accokeek, MD **❶**

Inside National Colonial Farm Visitor Center

☐ Piscataway Park/Accokeek, MD **❷**

Virginia

13 Arlington House, The Robert E. Lee Memorial

Part of the George Washington Memorial Parkway
McLean, Virginia
(703) 235–1530
www.nps.gov/arho

Number of cancellations: Nine: four for Arlington House, plus one for the Underground Railroad and cancellations at Arlington National Cemetery for four other parks

Difficulty: Easy

About this site: Colonel Robert E. Lee, who rose to the rank of general in the Confederate Army during the Civil War, lived here for thirty years with his wife and childhood sweetheart, Mary Anna Randolph Custis. The couple's wedding took place here in the family parlor, and Mary gave birth to six of their seven children in the dressing room next to the bedroom she shared with her husband. This is the home in which Lee made his decision to resign from the United States Army and join the Confederate cause in April 1861, writing his resignation letter in a bedroom on the second floor. Oddly enough, the house was actually constructed as a monument to President George Washington by Lee's father-in-law, George Washington Parke Custis, a stepson of the nation's first president.

❶ Don't miss this! This house still possesses many of the original furnishings and decorations used by the Custis and Lee families—most notably, the bed in Colonel and Mrs. Lee's bedroom and the chair in which Lee sat when he wrote his resignation letter to the United States Secretary of War on April 20, 1861. Many of the paintings throughout the house are Mary Lee's work, while others were painted by her father, including a large work that depicts Washington at the Battle of Monmouth.

Hours: Arlington House and bookstore are open daily from 9:30 A.M. to 4:30 P.M. They are closed Christmas and New Year's Day. The Arlington National Cemetery Bookstore is open 365 days a year. From April 1 to September 30, hours are from 8:00 A.M. to 7:00 P.M.; from October 1 to March 31, hours are from 8:00 A.M. to 5:00 P.M.

Fees: Admission to this park is free.

How to get there: The memorial is accessible by Tourmobile shuttle bus or by a ten-minute walk from the Arlington National Cemetery Visitor Center and parking area. Access from Washington, D.C., is via the Memorial Bridge. Access from Virginia is from the George Washington Memorial Parkway.

Metro: Use the Blue Line.

Stamping Locations and What the Cancellations Say

Inside Arlington House

☐ Arlington House, the Robert E. Lee Memorial/Arlington, VA ①

Arlington National Cemetery Bookstore
(703) 557–1713

☐ Arlington House/Arlington, VA ⑩

☐ GEORGE WASHINGTON MEMORIAL PARKWAY/ ARLINGTON, VA ①

☐ LYNDON BAINES JOHNSON MEMORIAL GROVE/ ARLINGTON, VA ①

☐ Theodore Roosevelt Island/Arlington, VA ①

☐ US Marine Corps Memorial/Arlington, VA ①

George Washington Memorial Parkway: Turkey Run Park Headquarters*

☐ Arlington House, Robert E. Lee Memorial/Arlington, VA ①

Arlington House Bookstore
Located behind house

☐ Arlington House/Arlington, VA ⑩

☐ Arlington House, R.E. Lee MEM/Underground RR Freedom Network ①

14 Claude Moore Colonial Farm

Part of George Washington Memorial Parkway
McLean, Virginia
(703) 442–7557
www.nps.gov/clmo

Number of cancellations: One

Difficulty: Tricky

About this site: With all of the sprawling plantations and mansions preserved throughout the national park system, Claude Moore Farm stands out because of its unique profile: It's a poor family's farm, circa 1771, where Moore and his family cultivated twelve acres of basic crops—tobacco, wheat, barley, corn, and other grains—with their hands and hoes. Visitors meet staff members in eighteenth-century garb who answer questions and respond to conversation as if the date really were 1771 and you're a neighbor or passerby from the same time period. These staff members actually work the farm just as Moore did, allowing livestock free run of the property and cooking meals at the log cabin's modest hearth.

Stamping tips: The site's limited hours make collecting this cancellation just a little tricky, but if you visit on a weekend, you will have no trouble getting it.

The park closes from mid-December through the end of March. However, the farm holds a clean-up weekend in mid-March to which families are invited (to volunteer and help get the farm ready for spring), so if you're passing through on that weekend, you may be able to wangle a cancellation. But in return, be prepared to pitch in! Bring your work gloves and have a real, authentic, eighteenth-century experience while you're earning your cancellation.

🛈 **Don't miss this!** Don't be shy! Walk up and talk to the farm family as they work in the fields or manage their livestock. They may hand you a hoe or ask you to help with carding wool or pulling weeds, so be ready to participate. You're sure to learn something you didn't know about the way the common people lived in a time when the wealthy owned slaves to do what the Moore family did for themselves. Farm management suggests a visit of an hour or less, which is just enough time to enjoy the characterizations created by the people who actually work this soil today.

If you've never experienced this kind of reenactment, keep in mind that any mention of modern-day farming equipment, television, or today's headlines will be met by blank stares and polite murmurings of, "I'm sorry, I don't know what you mean." It's a lot more fun to join the eighteenth-century timeline and ask questions about what you see and hear at the farm.

Hours: The farm is open from April 1 through mid-December, Wednesday through Sunday, from 10:00 A.M. to 4:30 P.M. It is closed Monday, Tuesday, and Thanksgiving.

The Gate House Shop is open April 1 through mid-December, Wednesday through Sunday, from 10:00 A.M. to 5:00 P.M. It is also closed Monday, Tuesday, and Thanksgiving.

Fees: $3.00 for adults; $2.00 for children three to twelve years old and senior citizens; free to children two and under.

How to get there: From Virginia, follow the Washington Beltway/Interstate 495 to Virginia 193 (Georgetown Pike). Go east toward Langley; drive 2.3 miles and turn left onto Colonial Farm Road, just prior to the junction with Virginia 123. Follow signs to the visitor parking lot.

From Washington, D.C., take the George Washington Memorial Parkway north to the exit for VA 123 toward McLean. Drive almost 1 mile and turn right onto VA 193; make the first right onto Colonial Farm Road and follow signs to the visitor parking lot.

Stamping Locations and What the Cancellations Say

Gate House Shop (gift shop)
(703) 903–9330

☐ Claude Moore Colonial Farm/McLean, VA ⓤ

🔢 George Washington Memorial Parkway

McLean, Virginia
(703) 289–2500
www.nps.gov/gwmp

Number of cancellations: Three for the parkway. You'll find four additional cancellations at Arlington National Cemetery, and fourteen additional cancellations at the parkway headquarters in Turkey Run Park.

Difficulty: Easy

About this site: This picturesque roadway not only protects a swath of natural land along the Potomac River, it also serves as one more remembrance of the father of our country and first president of the United States, George Washington. As such, it links a number of sites made famous by Washington's deeds at each: Mount Vernon, his home; the District of Columbia and the nation's capital, founded by Washington; and the Great Falls of the Potomac, where Washington began to realize his dream of making the entire Potomac River navigable by building the Patowmack Canal. Between these landmarks, the parkway winds past more than a dozen historic and park sites, including Glen Echo Park, Clara Barton National Historic Site, Dyke Marsh, Fort Hunt Park, Turkey Run Park, and the Women in Military Service for America Memorial, among many others.

Don't miss this! Most of the landmarks along the parkway are already highlighted in this book, but Dyke Marsh deserves a special mention here. This is the largest remaining piece of freshwater tidal wetland in the area, and scientists believe it formed as much as 7,000 years ago. Attempts to contain and drain the marsh in the 1800s and again in the 1950s and 1960s have left just a fraction of the original wetland intact. Nonetheless, the marsh holds its own as a prime habitat for birds and animals, even as non-native plants threaten to smother the floodplain. Stop and walk along the "haul road" here to view wildlife and see what efforts to revitalize this marsh have managed to accomplish.

Hours: The parkway is open twenty-four hours a day, seven days a week, 365 days a year.

The Turkey Run Park Ranger Station is open daily, sunrise to sunset.

The Turkey Run Park Headquarters of the George Washington Memorial Parkway is open Monday to Friday from 7:45 A.M. to 4:15 P.M.; it is closed on all federal holidays.

Arlington National Cemetery Bookstore is open every day of the year. Hours from April 1 to September 30 are from 8:00 A.M. to 7:00 P.M.; from October 1 to March 31, from 8:00 A.M. to 5:00 P.M.

Fees: Admission to the park is free.

How to get there: The parkway is adjacent to the Potomac River north and south of Washington, D.C., and is accessible from all major travel routes from the south and west of Washington, including Interstates 495, 95, and 66.

Turkey Run Park is located in McLean, Virginia, 2 miles off the Capital Beltway (I–495) on the George Washington Memorial Parkway (GWMP). From Beltway exit 43 (old exit 14), follow the GWMP 2 miles to the Turkey Run Park exit on the right. Follow signs into the park.

From Washington, D.C., and Old Town Alexandria, take the GWMP north approximately 8 miles and exit right at the Turkey Run Park sign. Make the first right turn into the park.

To reach Arlington National Cemetery from the Lincoln Memorial, take the Arlington Memorial Bridge across the Potomac River and continue to drive straight on Memorial Avenue into the cemetery.

Metro: Arlington National Cemetery station.

Stamping Locations and What the Cancellations Say

George Washington Memorial Parkway: Turkey Run Park Ranger Station

☐ George Washington Memorial Parkway/McLean, VA **Ⓓ**

George Washington Memorial Parkway: Turkey Run Park Headquarters*

☐ George Washington Memorial Parkway/McLean, VA **Ⓓ**

Arlington National Cemetery Bookstore

☐ GEORGE WASHINGTON MEMORIAL PARKWAY/ ARLINGTON, VA **Ⓤ**
☐ Arlington House/Arlington, VA **Ⓓ**
☐ LYNDON BAINES JOHNSON MEMORIAL GROVE/ ARLINGTON, VA **Ⓤ**
☐ Theodore Roosevelt Island/Arlington, VA **Ⓤ**
☐ US Marine Corps Memorial/Arlington, VA **Ⓤ**

16 Great Falls Park

Part of George Washington Memorial Parkway
McLean, Virginia
(703) 285–2965
www.nps.gov/grfa

Number of cancellations: Two, plus one for George Washington Memorial Parkway. Ten other cancellations are available at the parkway's Turkey Run Park headquarters.

Difficulty: Easy

About this site: If you've been touring Washington's many recreational and military parks and you're wishing for some really exciting natural scenery, Great Falls Park will satisfy your craving. Here the Potomac River drops 76 feet in less than a mile, creating a frothy cascade that barrels into Mather Gorge. The unusually hard igneous and metamorphic rock found here resists rapid erosion, creating jagged formations and high cliff edges that make the falling water just that much more dramatic. The most remarkable sight, however, is actually manmade: the remains of the Patowmack Canal, a brainchild of President George Washington and part of his dream to make the entire Potomac River navigable by bypassing the rushing falls.

Don't miss this! The Patowmack Canal Trail, a 0.75-mile mostly level hiking trail, reveals the remains of the dry laid stone walls and the locks that made this canal a critically important cargo route from 1802 until 1828. The trail takes hikers past the five locks—some original and some restored—that stepped barges down the mile-long, 76-foot drop that paralleled the Great Falls. Planning, engineering, and constructing this extraordinary waterway took seventeen years, far longer than planned—and keeping the entire structure in good working condition eventually bankrupted the Patowmack Company, the canal's oversight organization. But in its heyday, this canal carried thousands of boats with cargoes of whiskey, flour, tobacco, minerals, firearms, and cloth. Today, Washington's dream is a National Historic Landmark, a tribute to the laborers, indentured servants, and rented slaves who built this improbable waterway.

Hours: From November to mid-April the park is open daily from 10:00 A.M. to 4:00 P.M.; it is closed Christmas. From mid-April to

October, it is open Monday to Friday from 10:00 A.M. to 5:00 P.M.; Saturday and Sunday from 10:00 A.M. to 6:00 P.M.

Fees: Admission is $5.00 per vehicle, good for three days, or $3.00 per individual arriving on foot, horseback, motorcycle, or bicycle, good for three days.

How to get there: From Interstate 495, take exit 44 onto Virginia 193, also named Georgetown Pike. Take VA 193 west. Turn right at Old Dominion Drive (approximately 4.5 miles). Continue straight 1 mile to the entrance station.

Stamping Locations and What the Cancellations Say

Great Falls Park Visitor Center

☐ George Washington Memorial Parkway/McLean, VA **ⓓ**

☐ Great Falls Park/Great Falls, VA **ⓤ**

George Washington Memorial Parkway: Turkey Run Park Headquarters*

☐ GREAT FALLS PARK/GREAT FALLS, VA **ⓤ**

17 Lyndon Baines Johnson Memorial Grove on the Potomac

McLean, Virginia
(703) 289–2500
www.nps.gov/lyba

Number of cancellations: Three for the park. Four additional cancellations are available at Arlington National Cemetery.

Difficulty: Easy

About this site: A president with an unwavering devotion to the environment and to the beauty of the American landscape in all its forms, Lyndon Baines Johnson received this living tribute to his presidency in 1976, three years after his death. While his term in office bore the scars of the escalating war in Vietnam, Johnson is best remembered both for his environmental programs and for his advocacy of the Civil Rights Bill, which was signed into law in 1964 during the first year of his presidency and granted equal rights to Americans of every race and background for the first time in our nation's history. This fundamental, positive change in the American way of life secured Johnson's legacy as a great president, and his most dynamic statements are etched here in granite against a backdrop of thousands of flowering trees, bushes, and shrubs.

Don't miss this! While flowers bloom in this grove throughout the spring, summer, and fall, the best time to visit is during the early spring, when rhododendrons, azaleas, and daffodils are all at their peak. Combine this with the cherry blossoms along the National Mall, and you'll see some of the most delightful cultivated landscapes in the Washington, D.C., area.

Hours: LBJ Grove is open daily during daylight hours.

The George Washington Memorial Parkway: Turkey Run Park Ranger Station is open daily in spring, summer, and fall. However, the rangers are often in the field conducting educational programs or otherwise away, so this station will most likely be closed and locked during the park's busiest months (spring, summer, and fall), even though it is officially open during these times.

Arlington National Cemetery Bookstore opens daily at 8:00 A.M. From April 1 to September 30, the cemetery closes at 7:00 P.M. From October 1 to March 31, the cemetery closes at 5:00 P.M.

Fees: Admission to this park is free.

How to get there: The LBJ Memorial Grove is located in Lady Bird Johnson Park, on an island in the Potomac River near the Pentagon and Arlington National Cemetery. The George Washington Memorial Parkway provides direct access to the LBJ Grove parking areas. The grove is accessible from all major travel routes from the south and west of Washington, including Interstates 495, 395, and 66.

Stamping Locations and What the Cancellations Say

George Washington Memorial Parkway: Turkey Run Park Ranger Station
(703) 289–2552

☐ Lyndon B Johnson Memorial Grove/Washington DC ❶

George Washington Memorial Parkway: Turkey Run Park Headquarters*

☐ Lyndon B Johnson Memorial Grove/Washington D.C. ❶

Arlington National Cemetery Bookstore
(703) 557–1713

☐ LYNDON BAINES JOHNSON MEMORIAL GROVE/
  ARLINGTON, VA **Ⓤ**

☐ Arlington House/Arlington, VA **Ⓓ**

☐ GEORGE WASHINGTON MEMORIAL PARKWAY/
  ARLINGTON, VA **Ⓤ**

☐ Theodore Roosevelt Island/Arlington, VA **Ⓤ**

☐ US Marine Corps Memorial/Arlington, VA **Ⓤ**

🔢 U.S. Marine Corps Memorial/Netherlands Carillon

Part of George Washington Memorial Parkway
Arlington, Virginia
(703) 289–2500
www.nps.gov/gwmp/usmc.htm; www.nps.gov/gwmp/carillon.htm

Number of cancellations: Three for the memorial, plus four additional cancellations at the Arlington National Cemetery Bookstore

Difficulty: Easy

About this site: Dedicated to every Marine who died defending the United States since 1775, this memorial captures one moment in the courageous history of the U.S. Marine Corps: the raising of a large flag on February 23, 1945, as Marines captured Mount Suribachi on the tiny island of Iwo Jima. Joe Rosenthal, a news photographer embedded in the South Pacific with the American troops, immortalized this moment in a Pulitzer Prize–winning photograph that now stands as a symbol of American bravery and heroism in every conflict, from the Pacific Rim to New York City. To this day, a cloth flag flies from the bronze statue's 60-foot flagpole from dawn to dusk.

❗ Don't miss this! A gift of the Netherlands to the United States as a tribute to America's role in liberating the Netherlands from German occupation during World War II, the 127-foot-high carillon houses fifty bells—weighing thirty tons in all—that are played in special programs on May 5 (Dutch Independence Day), July 4, September 2, Thanksgiving Day, and December 21. Eighteen bells play American songs of patriotism and military marches at noon and 6:00 P.M. daily, with songs programmed by computer for the enjoyment of passers-by.

Hours: The memorial and the carillon are accessible twenty-four hours a day, seven days a week.

The George Washington Memorial Parkway's Turkey Run Park Ranger Station is open daily in spring, summer, and fall. However, the rangers are often in the field, so this station will most likely be closed and locked during the park's busiest months (spring, summer, and fall), even though it is officially open during these times.

Arlington National Cemetery Bookstore opens daily at 8:00 A.M. From April 1 to September 30, the cemetery closes at 7:00 P.M. From October 1 to March 31, the cemetery closes at 5:00 P.M.

Fees: Admission to this park is free.

How to get there: The memorial is located northwest of Arlington National Cemetery, off of Marshall Drive. From Interstate 66, cross the Potomac River on the Theodore Roosevelt Memorial Bridge and continue to Meade Street (left). Meade ends at Marshall Street; turn left. The Netherlands Carillon will be on your left; pass the carillon and turn left at the entrance to the U.S. Marine Corps Memorial.

Stamping Locations and What the Cancellations Say

George Washington Memorial Parkway: Turkey Run Park Ranger Station
(703) 289–2552

☐ Marine Corps Memorial/Netherlands Carillon/Arlington, VA ⓓ

Arlington National Cemetery Bookstore
(703) 557–1713

☐ US Marine Corps Memorial/Arlington, VA ⓤ

☐ Arlington House/Arlington, VA ⓓ

☐ GEORGE WASHINGTON MEMORIAL PARKWAY/ ARLINGTON, VA ⓤ

☐ LYNDON BAINES JOHNSON MEMORIAL GROVE/ ARLINGTON, VA ⓤ

☐ Theodore Roosevelt Island/Arlington, VA ⓤ

George Washington Memorial Parkway: Turkey Run Park Headquarters*

☐ Marine Corps Memorial/Netherlands Carillon/Arlington, VA ⓿

🔟 Women in Military Service for America Memorial

Part of George Washington Memorial Parkway
Arlington, Virginia
(703) 289–2500
www.nps.gov/gwmp/wimsa.htm

Number of cancellations: One (ten other cancellations are available at the stamping site at Turkey Run Park headquarters)

Difficulty: Easy

About this site: More than two million women have served in our nation's military since the American Revolution, and this memorial pays tribute to these courageous, dedicated women—many of whom have gone uncelebrated for decades. Here visitors can learn about the most distinguished of these women, including recipients of America's highest military honors, and view a film presentation on women's critical roles in wartime. Architects Marion Gail Weiss and Michael Manfredi worked with the existing hemicycle, a concrete and granite structure originally constructed as a ceremonial entrance to Arlington National Cemetery (but never used for this purpose), and added an exhibition hall with sixteen display alcoves, a 196-seat theater, and a Hall of Honor.

Stamping tips: While the memorial has its own gift shop, it does not have a cancellation on premises, so be sure to stop at George Washington Memorial Parkway: Turkey Run Park Headquarters to get the cancellation there.

🛑 **Don't miss this!** Inside the memorial, visit the interactive, computerized register to view the complete military service record of a friend or family member—or your own. More than 250,000 women in the military are listed here, and twelve computer terminals make this information easy to access. Even if you don't know a woman with a military record, pick someone at random and see what women have accomplished in domestic service and overseas, in wartime and in peace.

Hours: The memorial is open 8:00 A.M. to 5:00 P.M. from October 1 to March 31, and 8:00 A.M. to 7:00 P.M. from April 1 to September 30. It is closed on Christmas.

Arlington National Cemetery Bookstore opens daily at 8:00 A.M. From April 1 to September 30, the cemetery closes at 7:00 P.M. From October 1 to March 31, the cemetery closes at 5:00 P.M.

Fees: Admission to the memorial is free.

How to get there: To reach the memorial from Washington, D.C., cross the Fourteenth Street Bridge and follow Interstate 395 south to exit 8B (Virginia 110) north toward Rosslyn. Take the exit for Arlington National Cemetery. At the stop sign make a left onto Memorial Drive and the cemetery guards will direct you from there.

Stamping Locations and What the Cancellations Say

George Washington Memorial Parkway: Turkey Run Park Headquarters*

☐ Women In Military Service for America Memorial/ Arlington, VA ⓪

Washington, D.C.

20 African American Civil War Memorial

Part of National Mall & Memorial Parks
(202) 667–2267
www.nps.gov/afam

Number of cancellations: Two for this park; three more cancellations available at Ford's Theatre

Difficulty: Easy

About this site: The names of all the black soldiers who served during the Civil War—209,145 servicemen in all—are etched into the steel that composes this memorial. The United States Colored Troops (USCT) stepped forward to fight on the side of the Union from 1861 to 1865 for the freedom of four million slaves, serving in segregated divisions and distinguishing themselves in battles from Chapin's Farm and Petersburg in Virginia to Blakeley in Alabama. In all, the USCT participated in a total of 449 engagements, including thirty-nine major battles, and their ranks made up 10 percent of the Union Army. This 10-foot-tall memorial, dedicated in 1998, is the first designed by a black sculptor to be placed on federal land in Washington, D.C.

Stamping tips: Beyond the fact that the African American Museum is closed on Sunday and open for more limited hours on Saturday, you should have no trouble getting these cancellations. Ford's Theatre closes during matinee performances on Thursday, Saturday, and Sunday afternoons, but performances are not year-round. Check the Web site at www.fordstheatre.org for days and times, or call the box office at (202) 347–6262.

❶ Don't miss this! If you're not familiar with the service of the USCT and you'd like to know more, the African American Civil

War Museum provides a great deal of insight into the little-known history of these courageous black regiments. Despite their willingness to fight alongside their white counterparts, these soldiers encountered the same prejudice and discrimination from the United States military that they experienced in their civilian lives—yet they persevered and played an instrumental role in winning freedom for black slaves throughout the divided nation.

Hours: The memorial is open to the public year-round.

The African American Civil War Museum is open Monday–Friday, 10:00 A.M.–5:00 P.M.; Saturday, 10:00 A.M.–2:00 P.M.; closed Sunday.

Ford's Theatre is open daily from 9:00 A.M. to 5:00 P.M. It is closed Christmas and during matinees and rehearsals. The theatre is closed through November 2008 for renovation; cancellations can be obtained across the street at Petersen House until renovations are complete.

Fees: Admission to this memorial is free.

How to get there: Interstates 66 and 395 provide access to the Mall from the south. Interstate 495, New York Avenue, Rock Creek Parkway, George Washington Memorial Parkway, and the Cabin John Parkway provide access from the north. I–66 and U.S. Highways 50 and 29 provide access from the west. US 50, U.S. Highway 1, and Maryland 4 provide access from the east. The memorial is located on the corners of Vermont and U Streets Northwest.

NOTE: Once you are in Washington, use of the Metro trains is highly recommended; this memorial has a stop on the Green Line.

Stamping Locations and What the Cancellations Say

African American Civil War Memorial Freedom Foundation and Museum

1200 U Street Northwest

☐ African American Civil War Memorial/Washington, D.C. **Ⓤ**

Ford's Theatre bookstore

☐ African American Civil War Memorial/Washington, DC **Ⓤ**

☐ Ford's Theatre NHS/Washington, D.C. **Ⓤ**

☐ National Mall & Memorial Parks/Washington, DC **Ⓓ**

☐ Petersen House/Washington, DC **Ⓤ**

21 Anacostia Park

Part of National Capital Parks–East
(202) 690–5185
www.nps.gov/anac

Number of cancellations: One

Difficulty: Tricky

About this site: One of Washington's most significant recreational park, Anacostia covers more than 1,200 acres and offers ball fields, basketball and tennis courts, pavilions for picnickers, a 3,300-square-foot pavilion for roller-skating and events, an outdoor swimming pool, an eighteen-hole golf course, three marinas, four boat clubs, and a public boat ramp—and still has room for an impressive list of wildlife and native flora at Poplar Point, a 60-acre natural area with wetlands, meadows, and thickets that provide habitat for birds, butterflies, reptiles, and amphibians.

Stamping tips: While the park is open daily, the headquarters office is only open on weekdays. Be sure to visit during the week to get the cancellation.

Don't miss this! It's important to note that while most of Anacostia Park has been preserved for nearly a century, some of the park consists of land reclaimed from use as a landfill and trash-burning site, a greenhouse and nursery operation, and other semi-industrial activities. The emphasis here is on games, sports, boating, and general recreation, with an admirable refurbishing of land parcels that could benefit from such work. This effort continues now with a development plan to clean up the pollution in the Anacostia River (if you go boating here, keep in mind that the river is currently unsafe for swimming).

Hours: The park is open daily. Closed Thanksgiving, Christmas, and New Year's Day. The office is open Monday through Friday from 8:30 A.M. to 4:00 P.M.

Fees: General admission to the park is free.

How to get there: From Baltimore–Washington Parkway/Maryland 295, follow the Baltimore–Washington Parkway south toward Washington, D.C. When the parkway intersects MD 295, follow the lanes to the left toward Interstate 495/Capital Beltway. Take the eastbound Pennsylvania Avenue exit. Take the first right onto Fairlawn Avenue. Go to the stop sign and turn right again on Nicholson Street to enter the park.

From Interstate 395, go north into Washington, D.C., toward the Southeast/Southwest Freeway. When the freeway splits, bear right toward Martin Luther King, Jr. Avenue. Take the Anacostia Park exit to the stop sign. Turn right onto Good Hope Road to enter the park.

From Suitland Parkway/South Capitol Street, follow the Suitland Parkway west toward Washington, D.C. Turn right at the traffic signal onto Firth Sterling Avenue. Take a left turn at the next traffic signal onto Howard Road. When you approach the Douglass Bridge, the lanes will split and the park entrance is to the right.

Stamping Locations and What the Cancellations Say
Anacostia Park office

☐ ANACOSTIA PARK/WASHINGTON, D.C. Ⓤ

22 Capitol Hill Parks

An NPS management system
(202) 690–5185
www.nps.gov/cahe

Number of cancellations: One

Difficulty: Tricky

About this site: The network of small parks between Second Street and the Anacostia River all fall under a management organization called Capitol Hill Parks. Designed as part of the grand plan for the nation's capital created by Pierre L'Enfant in 1790, this collection of parks includes triangles and squares throughout this section of the city that provide welcome green space between federal buildings, city streets, and heavily populated areas. The parks (none of which are national parks in their own right) include Lincoln, Folger, Stanton, and Marion Parks; the Maryland Avenue triangles; the Pennsylvania Avenue medians; squares and triangles including Seward Square, Potomac Avenue Metro stations, and Twining Square; and other inner-city triangles and squares.

Stamping tips: The stamping location for Capitol Hill Parks is only open on weekdays. However, this is a cancellation-rich stop, so it will be worth visiting during the week.

❶ Don't miss this! You'll need to keep an eye out to actually see the Capitol Hill Parks, as they are scattered throughout a fairly wide area and most are simply grassy squares with foliage and, in some cases, small monuments. As you walk through the city's eastern streets, watch for these small, landscaped oases between rows of high-rise apartment and office buildings and surrounding streetscapes.

Hours: For office hours, see the listing for National Capital Parks–East in the Special Stamping Locations section of this guide.

Fees: Admission to these parks is free.

How to get there: The parks are all located between Second Street Northeast and Second Street Southeast and the Anacostia River in the city of Washington, D.C.

Stamping Locations and What the Cancellations Say

National Capital Parks–East headquarters*

☐ CAPITOL HILL PARKS/WASHINGTON, D.C. **❶**

23 Carter G. Woodson Home National Historic Site

(202) 673–2402
www.asalh.org/WoodsonHome.html

Number of cancellations: One, plus one for Mary McLeod Bethune Council House

Difficulty: Tricky

About this site: The founder of the Association for the Study of Negro Life and History, Carter G. Woodson's many accomplishments include the establishment of Negro History Week, which has grown to become Black History Month; publication of two magazines that brought important aspects of African-American history to light; and making black history an academic discipline now offered in most colleges and universities. Woodson lived and worked in this row house from 1915 until his death in 1950, and the Association for the Study of African American Life and History (ASALH) continued to operate here until 1971. When disrepair and interior damage threatened to destroy this house, ASALH entered into a partnership with the National Park Service to preserve it as a National Historic Site. The house received its national park status on February 27, 2006.

Currently, this house stands in considerable disrepair, making it unsafe even to venture inside. There are no visitor facilities or tours here, and none are planned until the renovation is completed (possibly 2009 or 2010).

Stamping tips: The cancellation lives at the Mary McLeod Bethune Council House, but it may leave with rangers or other staff members for use at programs in conjunction with the Association for African American Life and History, which are offered occasionally (check the Woodson home Web site for details). Call before you visit to be sure that the cancellation will be available when you arrive. If you'd like to actualize your stamping experience, you can enjoy the exhibits about Woodson at the Bethune Council House, and then visit the Woodson house exterior.

The National Park Service is currently conducting architectural and historical analysis and research on the building to determine the extent of the damage caused by its thirty vacant years. When the research team completes its work, a schedule for renovation will be determined.

Don't miss this! Site manager Robert Parker reports that visitors can participate in programs at the Mary McLeod Bethune Council House, about 5 blocks from the Woodson home, to learn more about Woodson and his work. Educational materials are available at the Bethune site, and the staff members there can provide considerable information about the development of Black History Month and Woodson's many other accomplishments.

Hours: The site is not yet open to the public. The Bethune Council House is open year-round, Monday to Saturday from 10:00 A.M. to 4:00 P.M.

Fees: Admission to the Bethune Council House is free.

How to get there: From the National Mall, proceed north on Ninth Street Northwest. The Woodson house is on the right between P and Q Streets; the address is 1538 Ninth Street Northwest.

To reach the Mary McLeod Bethune Council House from Baltimore and the north, take the Baltimore–Washington Parkway south to New York Avenue. Take New York Avenue to Massachusetts Avenue. Turn right onto Thirteenth Street. Go one block and turn left onto N Street. Go another block and turn right onto Vermont Avenue. The site at 1318 Vermont Avenue is a half block up the street on the left.

From Virginia and the south, take Fourteenth Street to Thomas Circle. Go right off the circle onto Vermont Avenue. The house is one-and-a-half blocks beyond the circle on the left.

Street parking is limited to two hours on Vermont Avenue. There are several pay parking lots within one or two blocks of Thomas Circle.

Metro: McPherson Square stop, Orange and Blue Lines. From the station, walk north on Fourteenth Street to Thomas Circle. Go around the circle to the right. Turn right onto Vermont Avenue; the house is one-and-a-half blocks beyond the circle on the left.

Stamping Locations and What the Cancellations Say
Mary McLeod Bethune Council House

☐ Carter G. Woodson Home NHS/Washington, D.C. ⓞ

☐ Mary McLeod Bethune Council House NHS/ Washington, DC ⓞ

24 Chesapeake & Ohio Canal National Historic Park

(301) 739–4200
www.nps.gov/choh

Number of cancellations: One, plus a stamp for Potomac Heritage National Scenic Trail. The C & O Canal continues through Maryland in the Mid-Atlantic Passport Region as well.

Difficulty: Tricky

About this site: You're at the southern end of the Chesapeake & Ohio Canal, a 184.5-mile waterway that provided a transportation route from Washington to the Ohio Valley before railroads took over as the dominant means for transporting raw materials and products. Here in Georgetown, the canal expanded the city's ability to export goods to the rest of the country, making this a major outlet for many desirable commodities.

Stamping tips: The visitor center is closed on Monday, Tuesday, and Friday. Plan for a Saturday or Sunday stop if possible.

❶ Don't miss this! Here at the Georgetown end of the canal, you can ride an actual canal barge pulled by mules that walk along the towpath, just as it was at the turn of the twentieth century. The mules, by the way, are named Ellie, Ida, Frances, Lil, Ada, Molly, and Nell, and they lead very comfortable lives compared to the mules of yesteryear, who worked eight hours a day, every day, pulling 220-ton boats. Today's mules only work a few hours a day and a few days a week, and their boat weighs barely a tenth of the originals.

Much of the scenery along the canal edges has been preserved here—the old warehouse district still stands—so your ride has a sense of authenticity you don't often find along the old canal routes in the eastern United States. The boat rides are available Wednesday through Sunday during the summer months.

Hours: Open year-round Wednesday, Thursday, Saturday, and Sunday from 9:00 A.M. to 4:30 P.M. Hours can vary without notice; call to check before visiting.

Fees: Admission to the Georgetown unit of the C & O Canal NHP is free.

How to get there: From Interstate 66, take the U.S. Highway 29 exit and cross the Potomac River on US 29. Follow US 29 to the right beyond the river; it becomes K Street Northwest. Continue to Thomas Jefferson Street Northwest. Turn left on Jefferson Street and cross the canal to the Georgetown Visitor Center at 1057 Thomas Jefferson Street Northwest.

Stamping Locations and What the Cancellations Say
Georgetown Visitor Center
(202) 653–5190

☐ C & O Canal National Historical Park/Washington, DC ❶

☐ Potomac Heritage National Scenic Trail/Washington, DC ❶

25 Constitution Gardens

(202) 426–6841
www.nps.gov/coga

Number of cancellations: Three for the gardens. Four cancellations for other parks are available at the Lincoln bookshop, along with the Constitution Gardens cancellation.

Difficulty: Easy

About this site: Originally called Potomac Park, this fifty-acre landscaped area on the National Mall (near the Vietnam Veterans Memorial) was rescued from decades of use as a United States Navy office site by President Richard Nixon in 1971, who served in the "temporary" buildings that stood here during World War II. More than ten years later, President Ronald Reagan rededicated this park in honor of the bicentennial of the U.S. Constitution. The lake here provides much-needed habitat for several species of fish, and visitors can glimpse many urban animals—squirrels, raccoons, red fox, and beaver—in this setting.

Don't miss this! The Memorial to the 56 Signers of the Declaration of Independence stands on the island in the middle of Constitution Lake.

Hours: Constitution Gardens is open daily from dawn to dusk. While open on Christmas, no rangers are on site that day.

The Vietnam Veterans Memorial is open daily from 8:00 A.M. to 11:45 P.M.; closed on Christmas.

The Lincoln Memorial is open daily from 8:00 A.M. to 11:45 P.M.; closed on Christmas.

Fees: Admission to this park is free.

How to get there: Interstates 66 and 395 provide access to the National Mall from the south. Interstate 495, New York Avenue, Rock Creek Parkway, George Washington Memorial Parkway, and the Cabin John Parkway provide access from the north. I–66 and U.S. Highways 50 and 29 provide access from the west. US 50, U.S. Highway 1, and Maryland 4 provide access from the east.

Stamping Locations and What the Cancellations Say
Vietnam Veterans Memorial Information Kiosk

☐ Constitution Gardens/Washington, D.C. ❶

☐ Vietnam Veterans Memorial/Washington, D.C. ❶

Survey Lodge Ranger Station*

☐ Constitution Gardens/Washington, D.C. ❶

Lincoln Memorial Bookshop

☐ Constitution Gardens/Washington, D.C. ❶

☐ Lincoln Memorial/Washington, D.C. ❶

☐ Vietnam Veterans Memorial/Washington, DC ❶

☐ Korean War Veterans Memorial/Washington D.C. ❶

☐ National Mall & Memorial Parks/Washington, D.C. ❶

26 Department of the Interior

(202) 208–4749
www.doi.gov

Number of cancellations: One

Difficulty: Tricky

About this site: The headquarters of the National Park Service is at the United States Department of the Interior, the organization that manages one out of every five acres of land in the nation. This major oversight organization manages dams, reservoirs, parks, open land, national wildlife refuges, and the resources that provide nearly a third of the country's energy. The department has eight divisions, including the Bureau of Indian Affairs, the Bureau of Reclamation, the U.S. Geological Survey, the Minerals Management Service, the U.S. Fish and Wildlife Service, the Bureau of Land Management, and the Office of Surface Mining, as well as the National Park Service.

Stamping tips: Since September 11, 2001, security at all federal buildings has increased dramatically. While collectors were welcome to drop in at the Department of the Interior in days gone by, today you need the following information for the security guards at the door: THE DESK OF FRANCES A. CHERRY, PUBLIC INQUIRIES TECH, OFFICE OF COMMUNICATIONS—ROOM 1013.

Once you've gotten clearance from the guards, you will pass through a metal detector. (Leave your pocketknife and any other sharp metal objects in your car or hotel room.) The security guards will call Ms. Cherry, who will come down to the lobby and bring you the cancellation.

Don't miss this! The National Park Service Information Office is the central clearinghouse for the official map and guide brochures for every national park. While you can no longer visit the office and pick up the brochures you need, you may ask for them during your visit.

Hours: Ms. Cherry is available Monday–Friday, 9:00 A.M.–3:30 P.M. If she is not in, someone else from the National Park Service Information Center will come to the lobby and provide the cancellation. The office is closed on all federal holidays.

Fees: Admission to this office is free.

How to get there: From the National Mall, C Street Northwest is between the Ellipse and Constitution Avenue. Walk two blocks from the Mall on C Street Northwest to reach the Department of the Interior building at 1849 C Street Northwest.

Stamping Locations and What the Cancellations Say

National Park Service Information Center
Department of the Interior
☐ DEPARTMENT OF THE INTERIOR/WASHINGTON, DC ❶

27 District of Columbia World War Memorial

Part of National Mall & Memorial Parks
(202) 426–6841
www.nps.gov/nama

Number of cancellations: One, plus eighteen other cancellations at Survey Lodge

Difficulty: Easy

About this site: This locally significant memorial commemorates the residents of the District of Columbia who served in World War I. Dedicated by President Herbert Hoover on Veterans Day, 1931, this monument remains the only memorial to local residents on the National Mall.

Don't miss this! You won't be able to see it, but a list of the 26,000 District of Columbia citizens who served in the Great War is preserved in the cornerstone of this memorial.

Hours: The memorial is open daily from dawn to dusk.

Fees: Admission to this memorial is free.

How to get there: The memorial is on the Mall south of Nineteenth Street Northwest (West Potomac Park), slightly off of Independence Avenue and in a grove of trees.

Stamping Locations and What the Cancellations Say

Survey Lodge Ranger Station*

☐ District of Columbia World War Memorial/Washington, D.C. **❶**

28 Ford's Theatre National Historic Site

(202) 426–6924
www.nps.gov/foth

Number of cancellations: Two for Ford's Theatre, two for Petersen House, and three additional cancellations

Difficulty: Easy

About this site: On April 14, 1865, actor John Wilkes Booth shot President Abraham Lincoln at point-blank range in the president's box at Ford's Theatre. Booth leapt from the box to the stage, landing in the midst of the performance of *Our American Cousin,* and ran off (despite the fact that he broke his leg in the leap) as bedlam ensued inside the theater. Lincoln was transported to a bed in the Petersen Boarding House across the street, where he died early the next morning. This history-changing moment, one that happened just five days after the Civil War ended when General Robert E. Lee surrendered to General Ulysses S. Grant at Appomattox, had a significant impact on the course of Reconstruction of the southern states.

Stamping tips: Ford's Theatre was closed for renovations in June 2007 and is scheduled to reopen to visitors in November 2008. During this time, Passport cancellation stamps will be available at an interim bookstore at Petersen House, or from a ranger at Petersen House.

The cancellation referred to by Eastern National as the "HWLD" stamp—which stands for "House Where Lincoln Died"— appears and disappears at random from Ford's Theatre. As of this writing, Ford's Theatre staff members say the cancellation now lives in the ranger's office upstairs at the theatre, but while the theatre is closed, it should be at Petersen House. In the interest of maintaining a good relationship between Passport stampers and this park, I absolutely do not recommend any kind of aggressive approach to getting this cancellation (in fact, my husband and I got this cancellation with ease at the Ford's Theatre box office in 2000).

Ford's Theatre closes during matinee performances on Thursday, Saturday, and Sunday afternoons, but performances are not year-round, so check the Web site at www.fordstheatre .org for performance dates and times, or call the box office at (202) 347–6262. The theatre also closes to the public for on-stage rehearsals. In all cases, the museum is open to the public—you'll just miss out on seeing the theatre and the president's box.

Don't miss this! Ford's Theatre is an icon, one of a handful of sites at which seminal events dramatically changed the course of American history. Chances are, you first heard about Lincoln's assassination in kindergarten or even earlier, just as you heard about Columbus discovering America, the Pilgrims landing at Plymouth Rock, and—if you're younger than forty—Rosa Parks refusing to give up her seat on the bus. That's why you need to savor your visit here, to feel the awesome power of actually being in the building in which such an event took place.

Take some time to study the displays in the basement of the theater. The collection includes Lincoln's bloodstained clothing, the gun with which Booth shot him, and the flag that was draped on the president's coffin. The artifacts also tell the lesser-known story of the chase and capture of Booth's accomplices, and the comeuppance they received at the hands of the U.S. legal system and an infuriated nation.

Stand in the box in which Lincoln and his guests sat on the night of the assassination. You're placing your feet on the exact spot where this president had his last waking moment—the power of his presence and of the awesome turn of events seem to hover here. While you're standing there, think about the fact that the last words spoken on stage before Booth's shot rang out were the laugh-producing line, "You sockdologizing old man trap!" These are the last words Lincoln heard before he died! Booth planned the assassination so carefully that he used the laughter following this line as cover for the sound of his gunshot.

Cross the street and see the surroundings in which Lincoln breathed his last without ever opening his eyes, in a bed too small for his great height.

Ford's Theatre is a live, working theatre in which you can see performances of professionally produced musicals and plays with American themes. Closed for 103 years after Lincoln's assassination, the theatre reopened in 1968 with the mission of presenting excellent performances in recognition of Lincoln's appreciation and enthusiasm for the performing arts. Check the schedule at www.fordstheatre.org.

Hours: Ford's Theatre is closed for renovations until November 2008. Otherwise, Ford's Theatre National Historic Site and Petersen House are open daily from 9:00 A.M. to 5:00 P.M. They are closed on Christmas. The Main Viewing Area (theatre) closes to the public during matinee performances and daytime rehearsals.

Fees: Admission to Ford's Theatre and Museum and Petersen House is free. To see a play at Ford's Theatre, purchase tickets at the box office.

How to get there: Parking is severely limited in the downtown area. Ford's Theatre is located near the intersection of Tenth and E Streets in the northwest section of the city, a short walk from two Metro stops at Metro Center and Gallery Place, and a block north of the FBI building on Pennsylvania Avenue.

If you drive into Washington, D.C., from the west, take Interstate 66, U.S. Highway 50 or U.S. Highway 29. From the north, take Interstate 495, New York Avenue, Rock Creek Parkway, George Washington Memorial Parkway, or the Cabin John Parkway. From the east, take US 50, U.S. Highway 1, or Maryland 4. From the south, use Interstates 66 or 395.

Stamping Locations and What the Cancellations Say

Ford's Theatre bookstore
(202) 426–0179

☐ Petersen House/Washington, DC ❶

☐ FORD'S THEATRE NHS/WASHINGTON, D.C. ⓤ
☐ African American Civil War Memorial/Washington, DC ⓤ
☐ National Mall & Memorial Parks/Washington, DC ⓓ

Ford's Theatre ranger's office
(202) 426–6924
Located upstairs at the theater
☐ PETERSEN HOUSE/WASHINGTON, D.C. ⓤ
☐ House Where Lincoln Died/Washington, D.C. ⓤ
☐ National Mail & Memorial Parks/Washington, DC ⓓ

29 Fort Circle Parks

Part of National Capital Parks–East
(202) 690–5185
www.nps.gov/nace

Number of cancellations: One for Fort Circle, plus twelve other cancellations at National Capital Parks–East headquarters

Difficulty: Tricky

About this site: This network of forts protected Washington, D.C., from attacks throughout the Civil War by guarding bridges, waterway entries, and land routes along the border with southern Maryland. Now under the care of National Capital Parks–East, Fort Circle Parks includes Fort Mahan, Fort Chaplin, Fort DuPont, Fort Davis, Battery Ricketts next to Fort Stanton, Fort Carroll, and Fort Greble.

❶ Don't miss this! The Fort Circle Hiker-Biker Trail of the National Recreation Trail system, a 7.9-mile link between Forts Mahan and Stanton, provides a pleasant, vigorous walk or bike ride along the ridge that borders the Anacostia River. This urban trail crosses a surprising amount of green space as it follows old roadways through forests, stream valleys, and beds of wildflowers between forts, supplying a sampling of natural, semi-wild beauty and wildlife viewing that contrasts with the manicured lawns and still reflecting pools of the National Mall.

Hours: The trail is open daily from dawn to dusk. See the entries on the individual forts for their hours and seasons.

Fees: Admission to these parks is free.

How to get there: Access the Fort Circle Hiker-Biker Trail from Fort Mahan, Fort Dupont in the center, or Fort Stanton.

To reach Fort Mahan from downtown Washington, take New York Avenue to Florida Avenue. Turn right on Florida and drive until Florida becomes Benning Road. Fort Mahan is on the left.

To reach Fort Dupont from Benning Road, turn right on Minnesota Avenue to Randle Circle. Go left around the circle to the park.

Take the Metro Blue or Orange Lines to the Potomac Avenue Station on Minnesota Avenue. Transfer to the V4 or V6 bus along Minnesota Avenue Southeast.

Stamping Locations and What the Cancellations Say

National Capital Parks–East headquarters*

☐ FORT CIRCLE PARKS/WASHINGTON, D.C. ❶

30 Fort Dupont Park

Part of National Capital Parks–East
(202) 426–5961
www.nps.gov/fodu

Number of cancellations: Three for this park: An additional cancellation for Frederick Douglass National Historic Site is available with the Fort Dupont cancellation, and twelve more cancellations are at National Capital Parks–East headquarters.

Difficulty: Tricky

About this site: The earthwork wall that remains on this site fortified a portion of Fort Dupont, one of the Civil War Defenses of Washington that guarded against invasion of the Union's capital from 1861 to 1865. Precariously situated between Union and Confederacy territory when war broke out within days of President Abraham Lincoln taking his first oath of office, Washington, D.C., required a level of protection never before achieved in the United States. The guns at this fort protected the Navy Yard Bridge, a critically important land route into the city, and Fort Dupont became a haven for slaves fleeing from the southern states as they moved northward to join the "contrabands" in Washington and other hospitable Union cities.

Stamping tips: Take note that the activity center in Fort Dupont Park is closed. The cancellation is available at the Frederick Douglass National Historic Site and at National Capital Parks–East headquarters. Cancellations are not available at the activity center.

❗ **Don't miss this!** Today Fort Dupont Park serves as a sports center with tennis and basketball courts, a softball diamond, and an indoor ice-skating rink. If these activities are not what drew you to Washington, D.C., consider participating in a ranger-led workshop or nature walk. Free weekend jazz concerts are open to the public in summer.

Hours: Fort Dupont Activity Center is closed. The park grounds are open daily from dawn to dusk.

Fees: Admission to this park is free.

How to get there: From downtown Washington D.C., drive east on Pennsylvania Avenue Southeast and cross the Sousa Bridge. Turn left on Minnesota Avenue and proceed to Randle Circle. Turn right at the circle to the entrance at Fort Dupont Drive.

From Benning Road, turn right on Minnesota Avenue to Randle Circle. Go left around the circle to the park.

Take the Metro Blue or Orange Lines to the Potomac Avenue Station on Minnesota Avenue. Transfer to V4 or V6 bus along Minnesota Avenue Southeast.

Stamping Locations and What the Cancellations Say

National Capital Parks–East headquarters office*

☐ FORT DUPONT NP/WASHINGTON, DC **Ⓤ**

☐ FORT DUPONT PARK/WASHINGTON, D.C. **Ⓓ**

Frederick Douglass National Historic Site bookstore
(202) 426–5961

☐ FORT DUPONT PARK/WASHINGTON, D.C. **Ⓓ**

☐ FREDERICK DOUGLASS NHS/WASHINGTON, D.C. **Ⓓ**

31 Franklin Delano Roosevelt Memorial

(202) 426–6841
www.nps.gov/fdrm

Number of cancellations: Three for the FDR Memorial, and one for National Mall & Memorial Parks. There are eighteen additional cancellations at the Survey Lodge.

Difficulty: Easy

About this site: He served as our thirty-second president for twelve years, longer than any other president in history, winning four elections by creating programs that put people back to work during the Great Depression; repairing the nation's economy; creating a system of financial security for people in need; building parks, bridges, and roadways; and championing the American cause in a world war on the European and Asian Pacific fronts. No other president, before or since, accomplished as much for the people of America as Franklin Delano Roosevelt did—and all of it from a wheelchair, the result of a crippling attack of polio that stole his ability to walk when he was thirty-nine. This memorial, the largest and most extensive in Washington, captures the flavor of Roosevelt's presidency in four outdoor rooms, one for each term in office.

Don't miss this! As stunning as this memorial can be by day, the best time to see it is at night. The artists who created this granite and bronze masterwork clearly made the night lighting a high priority in its overall design. In particular, one of the rooms contains pillars with human handprints pressed into them; at night, the lighting installed in the floor makes these handprints seem embossed instead of embedded, bringing them forward for heightened drama. As the memorial is open and lighted until midnight, you have plenty of opportunity to have dinner, enjoy a concert or some of Washington's nightlife, and then return to the memorial to see it at its most magnificent.

Hours: The memorial is open daily year-round from 8:00 A.M. to midnight. It is closed on Christmas.

Fees: Admission to the memorial is free.

How to get there: Public transportation is highly recommended for touring the National Mall and its memorials, as parking is very limited. The Tourmobile stops at the FDR Memorial every few minutes throughout the day. If you use your car, the memorial is located on West Basin Drive. From the National Mall, drive south on Fifteenth Street until it becomes East Basin Drive. Follow this around the Jefferson Memorial to the FDR Memorial. Limited parking is available at the memorial.

Stamping Locations and What the Cancellations Say

Roosevelt Memorial Visitor Center
(202) 376–6704
- ☐ Franklin Delano Roosevelt Memorial/Washington, D.C. **◐**
- ☐ National Mall & Memorial Parks/Washington, DC **◐**

Survey Lodge Ranger Station*
- ☐ Franklin Delano Roosevelt Memorial/Washington, D.C. **◐**

32 Frederick Douglass National Historic Site

(202) 426–5961
www.nps.gov/frdo

Number of cancellations: Three for Douglass, plus two cancellations for Fort Dupont and one for the Underground Railroad. There are twelve additional cancellations at National Capital Parks–East headquarters.

Difficulty: Tricky

About this site: Freedom fighter, abolitionist, outspoken advocate for the rights of all individuals—black and white, male and female—and arguably the most famous African American of the nineteenth century, Frederick Douglass spent the last eighteen years of his life in the home he purchased in Washington, D.C., in 1877. While living here at Cedar Hill, Douglass continued to advocate for women's rights, and also served as U.S. marshall, recorder of deeds, and ambassador to Haiti.

Stamping tips: The park is open daily year-round, but two other stamping locations—Fort Dupont Activity Center and the National Capital Parks–East office—have tricky hours. The parks office is not open on weekends; the Fort Dupont center is open on different days in different seasons (Tuesday–Saturday in summer; Monday–Friday in winter) and is not open Sunday.

Don't miss this! The ranger-led tours here offer the best way to get to know Frederick Douglass, his ideals, and his long list of accomplishments. Take the tour and hear the stories of Douglass's struggle to end racial discrimination and about his partnership with the leading suffragists to win the right to vote for women of every color.

Hours: The site is open mid-October through mid-April from 9:00 A.M. to 4:00 P.M. daily, and mid-April through mid-October from 9:00 A.M. to 5:00 P.M. daily. It is closed on Thanksgiving, Christmas, and New Year's Day.

Fees: Admission to the park is free. There is a $1.50 service charge for reservations to tour the home. Rerservations are strongly recommended.

How to get there: From the Mall, travel south on Ninth Street to Interstate 395 north. Exit onto Interstate 295 south and cross the Eleventh Street Bridge. Exit onto Martin Luther King, Jr. Avenue. Turn left on W Street Southeast. Proceed three blocks to the visitor center parking lot on the right.

From Interstate 495/95/Capital Beltway, take exit 3 north onto the Indian Head Highway (Maryland 210), which becomes South Capitol Street. Bear right onto Martin Luther King, Jr. Avenue. Turn right on W Street Southeast and proceed to the visitor center parking lot on the right.

Metro: Take the Green Line to Anacostia Metro. Board the B2 bus and disembark at the Fourteenth Street stop, which is in front of the house.

Stamping Locations and What the Cancellations Say

Frederick Douglass National Historic Site bookstore
(202) 426–5961

☐ FREDERICK DOUGLASS NHS/WASHINGTON, D.C. **ⓓ**

☐ FREDERICK DOUGLASS N.H.S./WASHINGTON, D.C. **ⓤ**

☐ Frederick Douglass NHS/Underground RR Freedom Network **ⓤ**

☐ FORT DUPONT NP/WASHINGTON, D.C. **ⓓ**

☐ FORT DUPONT PARK/WASHINGTON, D.C. **ⓓ**

National Capital Parks–East headquarters*

☐ FREDERICK DOUGLASS NHS/WASHINGTON, D.C. **Ⓓ**
(There is a slight variation between the cancellation at the bookstore, which has periods in the abbreviation of N.H.S., while the two other cancellations do not.)

🟥33 George Mason Memorial

Part of National Mall & Memorial Parks
(202) 426–6841
www.nps.gov/gemm

Number of cancellations: One, plus eighteen additional cancellations at the Survey Lodge

Difficulty: Easy

About this site: You may never have studied the Virginia Declaration of Rights, the document that inspired Thomas Jefferson in his composition of the Declaration of Independence—but the Virginia declaration, penned by George Mason, articulated the idea that all people have "certain inherent rights…the enjoyment of life and liberty, with the means of acquiring and possessing property, and pursuing and obtaining happiness and safety." Mason's high ideals led him to become a delegate to the Constitutional Convention in 1787, but he refused to sign the finished Constitution because it did not call for an abolition of slavery.

❗ Don't miss this! Here's a piece of information you may not actually find at the memorial: Mason was one of the principal advocates for the addition of a Bill of Rights to the Constitution after the original document was ratified. In fact, the absence of these rights at the time of its ratification had a great deal to do with Mason's refusal to put his signature on the Constitution. The Bill of Rights, ratified on December 15, 1791, was based on Mason's original Virginia Declaration of Rights and added ten amendments to the Constitution, among which were these fundamental rights: the freedom of speech, the press, peaceful assembly, and religious worship; the right to bear arms; prevention of unnecessary search and seizure, cruel and unusual punishment, double jeopardy, and self-incrimination; and the guarantee of the right to due process under the law.

Hours: The memorial never closes.

Fees: Admission to the memorial is free.

How to get there: The memorial is located in East Potomac Park near the Jefferson Memorial. Public transportation is highly recommended for touring the National Mall and memorials, as parking is very limited. The Tourmobile stops at the Jefferson Memorial every few minutes throughout the day. If you use your car, the memorial is located on East Basin Drive. From the National Mall, drive south on Fifteenth Street until it becomes East Basin Drive. Follow this around to the Jefferson Memorial and the George Mason Memorial. Limited parking is available at the memorial.

Stamping Locations and What the Cancellations Say

Survey Lodge Ranger Station*

☐ George Mason Memorial/Washington, D.C. **❶**

34 Harmony Hall

Part of National Capital Parks–East
Fort Washington, Maryland
(202) 690–5185
www.nps.gov/haha

Number of cancellations: Two for Harmony Hall, plus twelve additional cancellations available at National Capital Parks–East headquarters

Difficulty: Tricky

About this site: This eighteenth-century Georgian house provides a fine example of period architecture and design. Acquired by the National Park Service in 1966 to preserve this rare remaining plantation house, Harmony Hall was so named by its owners, Mr. and Mrs. Walter Dulany Addison, because they lived in the home for two years with another newly married couple—Walter's brother and his wife—and enjoyed unexpectedly cooperative and pleasant relations with them. The house is not open to the public.

Stamping tips: I've listed Harmony Hall in Washington, even though the house itself is in Maryland, because there is no cancellation at the house and you can't take a tour of it. The cancellation resides at the magical National Capital Parks–East Headquarters, along with many other cancellations. This office is open weekdays only during business hours. A second cancellation is at the Fort Washington Park Visitor Center.

❶ Don't miss this! If you make the drive to Harmony Hall, you'll see one of the great early colonial plantation homes remaining in the southern United States. The house overlooks the Potomac River and is essentially unchanged from its original construction—the date of which is estimated to be 1766 by the National Park Service, though local lore suggests it may have been as early as the 1720s.

Hours: The house is closed to visitors.

Fees: No fee is charged to look at the house from the outside.

How to get there: If you'd like to take a look at the house from the exterior, it's located at 10511 Livingston Road in Fort Washington, Maryland.

From the Capital Beltway (Interstate 495), take exit 3A (Indian Head Highway) south. Follow Indian Head Highway (Maryland 210) south for approximately 4 miles and make a right onto Fort Washington Road. Make the next right turn onto Livingston Road. The house is on the left, next to Harmony Hall Regional Center.

Stamping Locations and What the Cancellations Say
National Capital Parks–East headquarters*

☐ HARMONY HALL/FORT WASHINGTON, MD **❶**

Fort Washington Park Visitor Center

☐ Harmony Hall/Fort Washington, MD **❶**

35 John Ericsson National Memorial

Part of National Mall & Memorial Parks
(202) 426–6841
www.nps.gov/joer

Number of cancellations: One, plus eighteen additional cancellations at Survey Lodge

Difficulty: Easy

About this site: Who would guess it? Captain John Ericsson, a Swedish immigrant, brilliant engineer, and nineteenth-century naval officer, is celebrated here for his invention of the screw propeller. While this may not seem to be a monument-worthy accomplishment at first blush, this invention revolutionized the concept of propulsion through water, improving naval ships' speed, efficiency, profile on the water (lowering it significantly), and durability. The ship he designed, the USS *Monitor,* incorporated not only the screw-propeller design, but also a revolving gun turret and full iron construction—giving the Union a significant advantage over the Confederacy's wooden boats in the Civil War.

❶ Don't miss this! Take the time to really look at this memorial and its rich detail, with symbols representing naval military service, labor, industry, and Ericsson's original and adopted countries, Sweden and the United States. Designed by J. E. Fraser, the memorial earned its place on a postage stamp in 1926, the year of its dedication by the Crown Prince of Sweden.

Hours: The memorial never closes.

Fees: Admission to the memorial is free.

How to get there: The monument is at Ohio Drive and Independence Avenue Southwest, at the southern end of the Twenty-third Street approach to the Lincoln Memorial.

Stamping Locations and What the Cancellations Say
Survey Lodge Ranger Station*

☐ John Ericsson Memorial/Washington, D.C. ❶

36 John Paul Jones Memorial

Part of National Mall & Memorial Parks
(202) 426–6841
www.nps.gov/nacc

Number of cancellations: One, plus eighteen additional cancellations at Survey Lodge

Difficulty: Easy

About this site: "Surrender? I have not yet begun to fight!" declared John Paul Jones to Captain Richard Pearson of the British Royal Navy in 1779, hoisting the Stars and Stripes over his ship, the *Bonhomme Richard,* capturing Pearson's ship, and earning his place as one of the greatest heroes of the Continental navy. Here Jones appears as a 10-foot-tall bronze, an apt representation of one of the bravest and most successful sea captains in the newly formed American navy.

Don't miss this! Be sure to walk all the way around this memorial to see the bas-relief in bronze of Jones commanding the *Bonhomme Richard* in the midst of battle. Cast by New York sculptor Charles H. Nieuhaus, this detailed depiction of courage in the heat of battle is as much fun as it is dramatic, showing a larger-than-life figure in surroundings that suit our fantasies of this great sea captain as much as they portray history.

Hours: The memorial never closes.

Fees: Admission to the memorial is free.

How to get there: The memorial is in West Potomac Park at the intersection of Independence Avenue and Seventeenth Street Southwest, at the north end of the Tidal Basin.

Stamping Locations and What the Cancellations Say
Survey Lodge Ranger Station*

☐ John Paul Jones Memorial/Washington, D.C. **ⓤ**

(202) 426–6905
www.nps.gov/kepa

Number of cancellations: Two, plus twelve additional cancellations at National Capital Parks–East headquarters

Difficulty: Easy

About this site: When Civil War veteran W. B. Shaw turned his hand to gardening in 1882, he started this haven for aquatic plants as a hobby—and soon found himself running a public garden with his daughter, L. Helen Fowler. Together they operated this exotic urban oasis for twenty-six years and developed several new varieties of water lily. In 1938, when Mrs. Fowler sold the property to the National Park Service, the gardens became a protected area devoted to the preservation and cultivation of aquatic plants. Kenilworth Marsh, a seventy-seven-acre wetland, struggles for survival in the wake of pollution, dredging, and filling activities involved in maintaining a landfill here until the 1970s, but the tidal marsh still provides important habitat for many bird, animal, and plant species that ordinarily would not thrive in an urban setting.

Don't miss this! The best time of year to see aquatic plants in bloom here is from May to September, but you'll find plenty to enjoy in these gardens at virtually any time of year. Walk the River Trail, a short (not quite a mile) hike along the edge of Kenilworth Marsh, to get the best view of the marsh and the wildlife you're likely to glimpse along the way. Watch for unusual wading birds like the American bittern, and for butterflies, frogs, turtles, opossum, and other marsh dwellers. Enjoy a spectacular view of the marsh and wildflowers from the Marsh Boardwalk along the Anacostia River.

Hours: The park is open daily from 7:00 A.M. to 4:00 P.M. It is closed Thanksgiving, Christmas, and New Year's Day.

Fees: Admission to the park is free.

How to get there: The entrance to the Aquatic Gardens is just west of Interstate 295 (Kenilworth Avenue), between Quarles and Douglas Streets, on Anacostia Avenue.

The entrance to Kenilworth Park (the recreation area) is at the westernmost end of Nannie Helen Burroughs Avenue Northeast, just off I–295 (Kenilworth Avenue), about 0.5 mile south of the Aquatic Gardens entrance.

Stamping Locations and What the Cancellations Say

Aquatic Gardens Visitor Center

1550 Anacostia Avenue Northeast

☐ KENILWORTH AQUATIC GARDENS/WASHINGTON, D.C. ❶

National Capital Parks–East headquarters*

☐ KENILWORTH PARK AND/AQUATIC GARDENS ❶

38 Korean War Veterans Memorial

(202) 426–6841

www.nps.gov/kwvm

Number of cancellations: Seven: three for the Korean War memorial, plus four cancellations for other parks

Difficulty: Easy

About this site: On June 25, 1950, the United States military entered into a police action to protect South Koreans living in democracy from Communist takeover by the North Korean government. Before the conflict ended, 54,246 Americans lost their lives in battle. As the memorial itself says, they "answered the call to defend a country they never knew and a people they never met." This ingeniously designed memorial portrays soldiers from the U.S. Army, Navy, Marine Corps, and Air Force working together, with the sandblasted images of more than 2,000 photographs permanently etched into the granite wall behind them.

❶ **Don't miss this!** On the opposite side of this memorial, the United Nations Wall lists the countries that sent troops to Korea in support of the effort to drive communism from the democratic half of the country. Many visitors to this monument may have no idea that the United States was part of a multination effort to defend South Korea, and that twenty-two countries from all over the world suffered losses there as well.

Hours: The memorial is open daily from 8:00 A.M. to midnight. It is closed on Christmas.

Fees: Admission to the memorial is free.

How to get there: The memorial is on Daniel French Drive near the Lincoln Memorial. Interstates 66 and 395 provide access to the National Mall from the south. Interstate 495, New York Avenue, Rock Creek Parkway, and George Washington Memorial Parkway provide access from the north. I-66, and U.S. Highways 50 and 29 provide access from the west. US 50, U.S. Highway 1, and Maryland 4 provide access from the east.

Metro: The Foggy Bottom station is located north of the memorial on the corner of Twenty-third and I Streets.

Stamping Locations and What the Cancellations Say
Kiosk near Lincoln Memorial

☐ Korean War Veterans Memorial/Washington, D.C. Ⓓ

Lincoln Memorial Bookshop
(202) 653–9088

☐ Korean War Veterans Memorial/Washington, D.C. Ⓓ
☐ Constitution Gardens/Washington, D.C. Ⓓ
☐ Lincoln Memorial/Washington, D.C. Ⓓ
☐ Vietnam Veterans Memorial/Washington, D.C. Ⓓ
☐ National Mall & Memorial Parks/Washington, D.C. Ⓓ

Survey Lodge Ranger Station*

☐ Korean War Veterans Memorial/Washington, D.C. Ⓓ

39 Lincoln Memorial

(202) 426–6841
www.nps.gov/linc

Number of cancellations: Seven: three for the Lincoln Memorial, and four stamps for other parks

Difficulty: Easy

About this site: Abraham Lincoln, the nation's sixteenth president, led the United States throughout the Civil War and freed more than four million black slaves with the stroke of a pen, delivering the Emancipation Proclamation in the midst of brother-to-brother battles in a divided nation. A common man who grew up in log cabins in the Midwest, and was later revered for his plain-speaking ability to navigate the choppy waters of politics, Lincoln became an icon for the equality and civil rights of all men, regardless of race, ethnic origin, or economic background. This monument to the nation's most beloved president is arguably the most famous and universally recognizable memorial in Washington, D.C.

① Don't miss this! Have you ever stopped to read and ponder the Gettysburg Address? The 286 words of the most famous presidential speech ever given are inscribed on the south inner wall of the memorial, and they have lost nothing of their power nearly 150 years later. Lincoln delivered this speech at the dedication of the National Cemetery at Gettysburg on November 19, 1863, and it has since become a succinct statement of the nature of freedom, democracy, and equality for people all over the world. Take a few minutes (Lincoln delivered it in three) to read the speech again, and consider it in context—not just in its Civil War setting, but also in relation to every war fought to free people from oppression. Here, in this marble chamber designed to resemble the Parthenon in Greece, Lincoln's words resound with the meaning they carry well beyond the moment they were spoken: his timeless call for "a new birth of freedom," and for "government of the people, by the people, for the people."

Hours: The memorial is open daily from 8:00 A.M. to midnight. Park rangers are on site every day except Christmas.

Fees: Admission to the memorial is free.

How to get there: Interstates 66 and 395 provide access to the National Mall from the south. Interstate 495, New York Avenue, Rock Creek Parkway, and George Washington Memorial Parkway provide access from the north. I–66 and U.S. Highways 50 and 29 provide access from the west. US 50, U.S. Highway 1, and Maryland 4 provide access from the east.

Metro: The Foggy Bottom station is located north of the memorial on the corner of Twenty-third and I Streets.

Stamping Locations and What the Cancellations Say

Kiosk at Lincoln Memorial

☐ Lincoln Memorial/Washington, D.C. ⓓ

Lincoln Memorial Bookshop

☐ Lincoln Memorial/Washington, D.C. ⓓ

☐ National Mall & Memorial Parks/Washington, D.C. ⓓ

☐ Korean War Veterans Memorial/Washington, D.C. ⓓ

☐ Constitution Gardens/Washington, D.C. ⓓ

☐ Vietnam Veterans Memorial/Washington, D.C. ⓓ

Survey Lodge Ranger Station*

☐ Lincoln Memorial/Washington, D.C. ⓓ

40 Mary McLeod Bethune Council House National Historic Site

(202) 673–2402
www.nps.gov/mamc

Number of cancellations: Two, plus a cancellation for Carter G. Woodson Home National Historic Site, and twelve additional cancellations at National Capital Parks–East headquarters

Difficulty: Tricky

About this site: The National Council of Negro Women (NCNW) made its home here with its founder, Mary McLeod Bethune, from the early 1940s through the 1960s. A teacher who established the Daytona Educational and Industrial School for Negro Girls in Daytona Beach, Florida (which later became Bethune–Cookman University), Bethune worked tirelessly for the advancement of black women and children. Her work expanded beyond her college and the NCNW to an appointment by President Franklin Roosevelt to the position of Director of the Division of Negro Affairs in the National Youth Administration. In all, Bethune served under four presidents, influencing legislation affecting women of all colors, and continued her human rights advocacy efforts until her death in 1955.

Stamping tips: The house is not open on Sunday; be sure to make this a Saturday stop if you're visiting on a weekend.

❗ Don't miss this! The floor plan has not changed since Bethune lived here, and many of the furnishings are original. The physical structure and decoration, however, pale in comparison to the work that took place inside these rooms, as the women of the NCNW influenced legislation to integrate blacks into the military and the public school system. Programs initiated here affected health care, employment, and the preservation of black women's activities in the twentieth century, much of which is housed on this site in the National Archives for Black Women's History. You'll find that the majority of what you'll see here is as it was when women met here in the 1940s, 1950s, and 1960s to change the course of civil rights.

Hours: The site is open year-round Monday to Saturday, 10:00 A.M. to 4:00 P.M.

Fees: Admission to the site is free.

How to get there: From Baltimore and the north, take the Baltimore–Washington Parkway south to New York Avenue. Take New York Avenue to Massachusetts Avenue. Turn right onto Thirteenth Street. Go one block and turn left onto N Street. Go another block and turn right onto Vermont Avenue. The site at 1318 Vermont Avenue is a half block up the street on the left.

From Virginia and the south, take Fourteenth Street to Thomas Circle. Go right off the circle onto Vermont Avenue. The house is one-and-a-half blocks beyond the circle on the left.

Street parking is limited to two hours on Vermont Avenue. There are several pay parking lots within one or two blocks of Thomas Circle.

Metro: McPherson Square stop, Orange and Blue Lines. From the station, walk north on Fourteenth Street to Thomas Circle. Go around the circle to the right. Turn right onto Vermont Avenue; the house is one-and-a-half blocks beyond the circle on the left.

Stamping Locations and What the Cancellations Say
Mary McLeod Bethune Council House

☐ Mary McLeod Bethune Council House NHS/Washington, DC ❶

☐ Carter G. Woodson Home NHS/Washington, D.C. ❶

National Capital Parks–East headquarters*

☐ MARY McLEOD BETHUNE COUNCIL HOUSE NHS/
WASHINGTON, D.C. ❶
(an oversized cancellation)

41 Memorial to the 56 Signers of the Declaration of Independence

Part of National Mall & Memorial Parks
(202) 426–6841
www.nps.gov/archive/coga
Number of cancellations: One, plus eighteen additional cancellations at the Survey Lodge
Difficulty: Easy
About this site: On August 2, 1776, the fifty-six representatives to the Second Continental Congress applied their signatures to the document they had voted to ratify on July 4, essentially declaring war on their not-so-benevolent parent country, England. In forming the free and independent United States of America, these fifty-six men demonstrated courage we can only imagine, for they committed treason against their ruler and set into motion a series of events from which America would emerge the strongest nation in the world. This act of bravery—not simply rebelling, but signing their names to the rebellion and inviting England's wrath against themselves, their homes, and their families—is honored with carvings of each signature in granite.

❶ **Don't miss this!** It's all too easy to stroll past this memorial without noticing it—it is a simple, curved installation of Minnesota granite that looks more like a seating area than a monument. But this is Washington, D.C., and no piece of stone or sculpture exists here by chance. You'll find the memorial across the wooden footbridge on the island in Constitution Gardens. Stop to read the last line of the Declaration of Independence, and note that the signatures are inlaid with gold leaf, making them shine in just about any weather.
Hours: The memorial never closes.
Fees: Admission to the memorial is free.

How to get there: The monument is located on the lake in Constitution Gardens, on Constitution Avenue between Seventeenth and Twenty-third Streets, at the foot of Twentieth Street Northwest.

Metro: Foggy Bottom stop.

Stamping Locations and What the Cancellations Say
Survey Lodge Ranger Station*

☐ MEM to the 56 Signers of the Dec. of Independence/ Washington, D.C. ❶

42 National Mall & Memorial Parks

(202) 426–6841
www.nps.gov/nama

Number of cancellations: Eight for the National Mall. Twelve cancellations for other parks are available at sites with National Mall cancellations. Eighteen additional cancellations are available at Survey Lodge.

Difficulty: Easy

About this site: National Mall & Memorial Parks is a management umbrella organization for all of the monuments, memorials, open spaces, and grounds in the general area of the National Mall. The Mall itself extends from Third Street (near the Capitol building) to Fourteenth Street, where the grounds surrounding the Washington Monument begin. In all, 156 spaces—including reservations, circles, fountains, and green areas—are managed by this organization, as are Ford's Theatre, Petersen House, Potomac Park, Hains Point, and Pennsylvania Avenue National Historic Site.

❶ **Don't miss this!** Cherry blossoms in spring—can we talk about Washington, D.C., without mentioning these? National Mall & Memorial Parks is the organization responsible for the care and feeding of the 3,700 Japanese cherry trees in the Tidal Basin, as well as for the 2,000 American elm trees that line the mall. A gift to the United States from the Vicountess Chinda of Japan and originally planted by First Lady Helen Taft in 1912, the cherry trees usually bloom between mid-March and mid-April. The two varieties bloom at slightly different times in spring, so even if you miss the peak days, you still may see masses of lovely pink blossoms.

Hours: The mall and memorials are open daily year-round. See entries for individual monuments and memorials for specific times. There are no rangers on duty on Christmas.

Fees: Admission to the Mall is free.

How to get there: Interstates 66 and 395 provide access to the Mall from the south. Interstate 495, New York Avenue, Rock Creek Parkway, George Washington Memorial Parkway, and the Cabin John Parkway provide access from the north. I-66 and U.S. Highways 50 and 29 provide access from the west. US 50, U.S. Highway 1, and Maryland 4 provide access from the east.

Metro: Smithsonian station.

Stamping Locations and What the Cancellations Say

Top of the Washington Monument

☐ National Mall/Washington, D.C. **❶**

☐ National Mall & Memorial Parks/Washington, D.C. **❷**

Ford's Theatre Bookstore

☐ National Mall & Memorial Parks/Washington, D.C. **❷**

☐ African American Civil War Memorial/Washington, DC **❶**

☐ Petersen House/Washington, DC **❶**

☐ FORD'S THEATRE NHS/WASHINGTON, D.C. **❶**

Ford's Theatre ranger's office
(202) 426–6924
Located upstairs at the theater

☐ National Mall & Memorial Parks/Washington, DC **❷**

☐ PETERSEN HOUSE/WASHINGTON, D.C. **❶**

☐ House Where Lincoln Died/Washington, D.C. **❶**

Franklin Delano Roosevelt Memorial Visitor Center

☐ National Mall & Memorial Parks/Washington, DC **❷**

☐ Franklin Delano Roosevelt Memorial/Washington, D.C. **❷**

Lincoln Memorial Bookshop

☐ National Mall & Memorial Parks/Washington, D.C. **Ⓓ**

☐ Lincoln Memorial/Washington, D.C. **Ⓓ**

☐ Korean War Veterans Memorial/Washington D.C. **Ⓓ**

☐ Constitution Gardens/Washington, D.C. **Ⓓ**

☐ Vietnam Veterans Memorial/Washington, D.C. **Ⓓ**

Thomas Jefferson Memorial Bookshop

☐ National Mall & Memorial Parks/Washington, D.C. **Ⓓ**

☐ Thomas Jefferson National Memorial/Washington, D.C. **Ⓤ**

Survey Lodge Ranger Station*

☐ National Mall & Memorial Parks/Washington, D.C. **Ⓓ**

43 Old Post Office Tower

(202) 606–8694
www.nps.gov/opot

Number of cancellations: One, plus a cancellation for Pennsylvania Avenue

Difficulty: Easy

About this site: Completed in 1899, the Old Post Office served the District of Columbia despite severe criticisms from the media and others about its architecture (described as "a cross between a cathedral and a cotton mill" by the *New York Times*). It stood as the largest building in the district at the time, and the first with a full electrical power plant, capable of powering 3,900 lights. Its granite outer skin covers a steel frame, also a first for Washington.

With all of its technological innovations, however, the post office became known as "old" just fifteen years after its construction, and an outcry to tear it down nearly brought this remarkable example of Richardsonian Romanesque architecture to the ground after the postal service moved out in 1934. Concerned citizens led by National Endowment for the Arts chairwoman Nancy Hanks saved the Old Post Office from demolition in the early 1970s, and the building now serves as federal office space with some public use areas.

Stamping tips: Watch out for those tricky Thursday nights, when the tower is closed for bell-ringing practice. But otherwise, you'll get this cancellation without special effort.

❶ Don't miss this! The short ranger-led program is a delight, ending with a view from the 270-foot-high, open-air tower observation deck and an opportunity to see the Bells of Congress, a gift from the Ditchley Foundation in England in celebration of the country's Bicentennial in 1976.

Even if you're skittish about heights, the view of our nation's capital from this level is worth the jitters. From above, the city comes together in a grand plan of smooth, green lawns, sparkling marble columns, and an intelligently planned network of streets and circles that make it all seem so logical. It's a picture we see so often on the nightly news, but so rarely of our own volition. Take the elevator up and let the ranger guide you through the rest.

Hours: From the first weekend in June through Labor Day, the site is open Monday to Friday from 9:00 A.M. to 7:45 P.M., and on Saturday, Sunday, and holidays from 10:00 A.M. to 5:45 P.M. From Labor Day through Memorial Day, the site is open Monday to Friday from 9:00 A.M. to 4:45 P.M., and on weekends and holidays from 10:00 A.M. to 5:45 P.M. It is closed Thanksgiving, Christmas, and New Year's Day.

The Old Post Office Tower is closed every Thursday evening from 6:30 to 9:30 P.M. for bell-ringing practice. The tower also closes for up to three hours for bell-ringing on federal holidays and other special occasions as designated by Congress.

Fees: Admission to the tower is free.

How to get there: The Old Post Office is located at the southeast corner of Pennsylvania Avenue and Twelfth Street Northwest. Limited on-street parking is available during non-rush times (9:30 A.M.–4:00 P.M.) on weekdays and all day on weekends and holidays. Parking may be restricted during special events. Several commercial parking lots are located near the building.

Metro: The Federal Triangle Station (Orange and Blue Lines) is directly across Twelfth Street from the Old Post Office.

Stamping Locations and What the Cancellations Say

Old Post Office Tower

Located in the lower level information station

☐ Old Post Office Tower/Washington, D.C. **❶**

☐ Pennsylvania Avenue NHS/Washington, DC **❶**

---

44 Pennsylvania Avenue National Historic Site

(202) 426–6841

www.nps.gov/paav

Number of cancellations: Two: one for Pennsylvania Avenue and one for Old Post Office Tower

Difficulty: Easy

About this site: Every four years the United States inaugurates a president on Pennsylvania Avenue, with parades and celebrations that fill the street with people and activity. This dependable historic event is only one of thousands that make this "America's Main Street": The avenue also hosts protest rallies and marches for every cause, parades honoring heroes from military leaders to astronauts, motorcades carrying visiting dignitaries and heads of state, funeral processions, and all manner of patriotic demonstrations. The White House, home of the president and the offices of the administration, is located at 1600 Pennsylvania Avenue; the street ends at the Capitol building.

❶ Don't miss this! The avenue's current condition as a center for government activity and commerce is actually a fairly recent development, as the Great Depression of the 1930s and the riots following Dr. Martin Luther King's assassination in 1968 spun this road into a downward spiral. Businesses destroyed by looting and burning fled the area, and banks turned down all requests for investment in the roadway, resulting in a 42 percent loss in shopping and other business traffic. President Lyndon Johnson formed a commission to revitalize the avenue, which resulted in the tree-lined boulevard filled with gleaming government buildings that we see today. By all means, take a stroll down this road to see a fine example of sustained urban renewal.

Hours: The avenue is open daily year-round.

Old Post Office Tower is open from the first weekend in June through Labor Day, Monday to Friday, from 9:00 A.M. to 7:45 P.M., and on Saturday, Sunday, and holidays from 10:00 A.M. to 5:45 P.M. From Labor Day through Memorial Day, the site is open Monday to Friday from 9:00 A.M. to 4:45 P.M., and on weekends and holidays from 10:00 A.M. to 5:45 P.M. It is closed Thanksgiving, Christmas, and New Year's Day.

The Old Post Office Tower is closed every Thursday evening from 6:30 to 9:30 P.M. for bell-ringing practice. The tower also closes for up to three hours for bell-ringing on federal holidays and other special occasions as designated by Congress.

Fees: There is no admission fee.

How to get there: Interstates 66 and 395 provide access from the south. Interstate 495, New York Avenue, Rock Creek Parkway, George Washington Memorial Parkway, and the Cabin John Parkway provide access from the north. I–66 and U.S. Highways 50 and 29 provide access from the west. US 50, U.S. Highway 1, and Maryland 4 provide access from the east.

Metro: Federal Triangle Station (Blue and Orange Lines).

Stamping Locations and What the Cancellations Say
Old Post Office Tower
Located in the lower level information station

☐ Pennsylvania Avenue NHS/Washington, DC ❶

☐ Old Post Office Tower/Washington, D.C. ❶

45 Potomac Heritage National Scenic Trail

(202) 619–7222
www.nps.gov/pohe

Number of cancellations: Two, plus a cancellation for C & O Canal National Historic Park

Difficulty: Tricky

About this site: This collection of scenic and historic trails winds for miles through Washington, D.C., Maryland, Virginia, and Pennsylvania. In the Capital district, the trail follows the Fort

Circle Parks route for 19.4 miles from Oxon Hill Farm to Fort DeRussy in Rock Creek Park, and then continues for another 5.6 miles to the Chesapeake & Ohio Canal Towpath.

Stamping tips: Limited hours at the Georgetown Visitor Center and weekdays-only hours at the George Washington Memorial Parkway headquarters make getting these cancellations a little tricky. Be sure to travel on a Wednesday or Thursday during the spring, summer, and early fall to land both cancellations in one trip.

❶ Don't miss this! The walk along the Fort Circle Parks trail segment provides you with a close-up look at the conservation efforts taking place along the Anacostia River, as well as the successful execution of a protection plan for this string of former Civil War forts. The Fort Circle creates a sort of greenbelt around the District of Columbia, an extended open space saved from development while preserving the historic buildings and grounds. Meanwhile, efforts to clean up the Anacostia River—long polluted by the rapid expansion of industry, waste management, and residential development that took place in the first half of the twentieth century—are resulting in the restoration of green spaces and wetlands along the river.

While the 19.4-mile hike is too long for most people, it transects residential neighborhoods and well-traveled roadways, so you have the option of walking portions of it and taking the Metro back when you've had enough. For a complete point-to-point description of the 19.4-mile walk and the 5.6-mile segment that follows the Fort Circle Parks trail, visit www.potomactrace.org/hikingguide/washdc.html#map.

Hours: The Potomac Heritage National Scenic Trail is open twenty-four hours a day, seven days a week, year-round.

The Georgetown Visitor Center is open Wednesday to Sunday only, 9:00 A.M. to 4:30 P.M.

Fees: Admission to this trail is free.

How to get there: From Interstate 66, take the U.S. Highway 29 exit and cross the Potomac River on US 29. Follow US 29 to the right after the river; it becomes K Street Northwest. Continue to Thomas Jefferson Street Northwest. Turn left on Jefferson Street and cross the canal to the Georgetown Visitor Center.

Stamping Locations and What the Cancellations Say

Georgetown Visitor Center
1057 Thomas Jefferson Street Northwest
(202) 653–5190

☐ Potomac Heritage National Scenic Trail/Washington, DC ❶

☐ C & O Canal National Historical Park/Washington, DC ❶

George Washington Memorial Parkway: Turkey Run Park Headquarters*

☐ Potomac Heritage/National Scenic Trail ❶

46 President's Park (White House)

(202) 208–1631
www.nps.gov/whho
Number of cancellations: Two
Difficulty: Easy

About this site: Every president of the United States (with the notable exception of George Washington) has lived in the White House since its construction was completed in 1800. Burned by the British in 1814, accidentally damaged by fire in 1929 during Herbert Hoover's presidency, gutted and renovated while President Harry Truman was in office, and redecorated in specific areas by each president and his wife to reflect their personal style, the White House takes on the personality of its residents while maintaining its own timeless majesty.

The residence alone contains 132 rooms on six levels, and accommodated the president's staff as well as the family and their guests until 1902, when President Theodore Roosevelt moved his staff into an addition that became known as the West Wing. The Oval Office, Roosevelt Room, Cabinet Room, and James Brady Press Briefing Room are all found in the West Wing, and the president's executive staff has its offices in this wing as well.

Stamping tips: These cancellations are easy to get, but don't wait until the end of the day, as both the visitor center and the Ellipse pavilion close by mid-afternoon.

If you take the White House tour, you'll need to leave a lot of the items you usually carry with you in your car, hotel room, or camper. Here's a list of prohibited items: handbags, book bags, backpacks, purses, food and beverages of any kind, strollers, cameras, video recorders or any type of recording device, tobacco products, personal grooming items (makeup, hair brush, comb, lip balm, hand lotions, etc.), any pointed objects (pens, knitting needles, etc.), aerosol containers, guns, ammunition, fireworks, electric stun guns, Mace, martial arts weapons/devices, or knives of any size. Essentially, carry your wallet and identification and leave everything else behind. The U.S. Secret Service runs the security at the tour entrance, and they have no sense of humor. Be sure to follow these directions without exception.

❶ **Don't miss this!** You can get the cancellation without taking the White House tour—but why on earth would you want to? The opportunity to walk through the rooms used by the president, the White House staff, and the other people who run our country is a heady experience, made even more dizzying by the chance that you just might catch a glimpse of the president or the first lady (or, someday, the first gentleman). No matter what your politics may be, it's not every day you can say that you shared floor space for a moment with the leader of the free world. The hallways hung with famous presidential portraits, the furnishings and accouterments chosen by first ladies two hundred years ago or as recently as this week, the knowledge that decisions affecting millions of people are being made in the next room . . . this is the White House, the nerve center of the United States of America. Make reservations at least a month in advance by calling (202) 456–7041, and for heaven's sake, take the tour!

Hours: The White House Visitor Center is open daily from 7:30 A.M. to 4:00 P.M. It is closed Thanksgiving, Christmas, and New Year's Day.

The Ellipse Visitor Pavilion is open daily from 8:00 A.M. to 3:00 P.M. It is closed Thanksgiving, Christmas, and New Year's Day.

Fees: Admission to the White House is free.

How to get there: Interstates 66 and 395 provide access from the south. Interstate 495, New York Avenue, Rock Creek Parkway, George Washington Memorial Parkway, and the Cabin John Parkway provide access from the north. I–66 and U.S. Highways 50 and 29 provide access from the west. US 50, U.S. Highway 1, and Maryland 4 provide access from the east. The White House itself is at 1600 Pennsylvania Avenue. On-street parking is not available near the White House, and use of public transportation is strongly encouraged.

Metro: Federal Triangle (Blue and Orange Lines), Metro Center (Blue, Orange, and Red Lines) or McPherson Square (Blue and Orange Lines).

Stamping Locations and What the Cancellations Say

White House Visitor Center

Located in the north end of the Department of Commerce Building between Fourteenth and Fifteenth Streets on Pennsylvania Avenue Northwest

☐ President's Park–The White House/Washington, DC ◑

Ellipse Visitor Pavilion

Located on the Ellipse south of the White House; the nearest intersection is Fifteenth and E Streets Northwest

☐ President's Park–The White House/Washington, D.C. ◑

47 Rock Creek Park

(including Peirce Mill Barn and the Old Stone House)
(202) 895–6070
www.nps.gov/rocr

Number of cancellations: Six

Difficulty: Challenging

About this site: Bisecting Washington, D.C., at twice the size of New York's Central Park, Rock Creek Park combines historic landmarks with recreational facilities and natural spaces to provide a popular place for District of Columbia residents to play. Like many other parks in and around Washington, this one is enjoying a conservational rebirth as a new management plan calls for the removal of old, disused drainage lines and fish barriers to help restore many species of fish to cleaner waters. The park provides historical perspective with the Old Stone House, an eighteenth-century common family dwelling, and Peirce Mill, the last remaining gristmill of eight that once dotted the banks of Rock Creek. Spectator sports, jogging and cycling trails, a nature center and planetarium, an outdoor concert venue, and picnic and playground facilities all draw crowds to this park every year.

Stamping tips: The only days that you can get all of the cancellations for this park in one visit are Saturday and Sunday, and then only in the afternoon from noon to 4:00 P.M., as Peirce Mill Barn maintains very limited hours. The nature center and Old Stone House are not open on Monday or Tuesday, so you need to plan your trip to Rock Creek Park within a tight weekend time frame to get the cancellations.

What's more, the Old Stone House is not actually in the park—it's located in Georgetown, just one block away from the Georgetown Visitor Center of the C & O Canal. You may want to plan on a Friday stop at Georgetown for the Old Stone House cancellation, as well as the C & O Canal and Potomac Heritage National Scenic Trail cancellations at the visitor center (and continue out to Theodore Roosevelt Island, which is nearby), and then head to Rock Creek Park on Saturday.

Don't miss this! If you're traveling with children, be sure to stop at the Nature Center and Planetarium, an educational and observation center created with young children as its audience. Its Discovery Room gives kids (and adults) the opportunity to touch and examine all kinds of natural objects found in the park, and there's a glass-faced beehive built into the back wall of the exhibit room where you can watch bees at work in complete safety.

Are you curious about Klingle Mansion, for which there's a cancellation at the nature center? It's the building that houses Rock Creek Park headquarters, and it's not open to the public. If you'd like to take a look at this old Peirce Plantation house from the outside, you'll find it at 3545 Williamsburg Lane Northwest, just north of the National Zoo.

Hours: The park is open during daylight hours, seven days a week.

The Nature Center and Planetarium are open Wednesday to Sunday from 9:00 A.M. to 5:00 P.M., and are closed New Year's Day, July 4, Thanksgiving, and Christmas.

The Old Stone House is open Wednesday to Sunday from noon to 5:00 P.M., and is closed New Year's Day, July 4, Thanksgiving, and Christmas.

Peirce Mill is closed for repairs until further notice. Peirce Barn is open Saturday and Sunday from noon to 4:00 P.M., and is closed New Year's Day, July 4, Thanksgiving, and Christmas.

Fees: Admission to the park is free.

How to get there: From downtown Washington, D.C., take the Rock Creek and Potomac Parkway north to Beach Drive. Exit onto Beach Drive north, and take it to Broad Branch Road; turn left and then right onto Glover Road. Follow the signs to the nature center.

NOTE: The parkway is one-way southbound on weekdays from 6:45 to 9:45 A.M. During this time, you can take Sixteenth Street to Military Road west, then turn left on Glover Road. The parkway is one-way north from 3:45 to 6:30 P.M. As an alternative, you can take Glover Road to Military Road east, then go south on Sixteenth Street to downtown.

Metro: Take the Red Line to either the Friendship Heights or Fort Totten Metro stops. Transfer to the E2 bus line, which runs along Military/Missouri/Riggs Road between the two stations. Get off at the intersection of Glover (also called Oregon) and Military Roads. Walk south on the trail up the hill to the nature center (approximately 100 yards).

Stamping Locations and What the Cancellations Say

Rock Creek Park Nature Center
5200 Glover Road Northwest
(202) 895–6070
Located 0.25 mile south of Military Road

☐ ROCK CREEK PARK, KLINGLE MANSION/
   WASHINGTON, D.C. **❶**

☐ Rock Creek Park Nature Center/Washington, D.C. **❶**

☐ ROCK CREEK PARK, OLD STONE HOUSE/
   WASHINGTON, D.C. **❶**

☐ Rock Creek Park Peirce Mill/Washington DC **❶**

Old Stone House
3051 M Street Northwest
(202) 426–6851
Located in Georgetown between Thirtieth and Thirty-first Streets

☐ ROCK CREEK PARK, OLD STONE HOUSE/
   WASHINGTON, D.C. **❶**

Barn at Peirce Mill
(202) 282–0927
Located on Tilden Street, just west of Beach Drive and east of
Connecticut Avenue

☐ ROCK CREEK PARK, PEIRCE MILL/WASHINGTON, D.C. ⓤ

48 Sewall–Belmont House National Historic Site

District of Columbia NPS Affiliated Site/Part of National Capital
Parks–East
(202) 546–1210
www.nps.gov/sebe

Number of cancellations: Two, plus twelve additional cancellations at National Capital Parks–East headquarters

Difficulty: Tricky

About this site: Since 1929, this house—built by Robert Sewall in 1799 and purchased for its ultimate purpose by Alva Belmont—has served as the headquarters of the National Woman's Party (NWP). Formed in 1916 when its leader, Alice Paul, split from another women's rights group because her tactics seemed "too extreme" to them, the NWP quickly rose to lead the campaign for equal rights for women. Paul targeted the White House and Congress and led nonviolent, highly dramatic protests in Washington—from marches with colorful suffrage banners to daily picketing in front of the White House—for which she and her comrades were arrested and brutalized in prison.

Once released, Paul took her campaign to the people through speaking opportunities and the media, creating overwhelming public support for women's suffrage. She and her comrades finally succeeded when Congress passed the Susan B. Anthony Amendment (the Nineteenth Amendment to the Constitution) in 1920, giving women the right to vote.

Stamping tips: With its limited hours and a required one-hour guided tour, Sewall–Belmont House is a tricky stop, so be sure to allow enough time at the right time to visit here and get the cancellation.

❶ **Don't miss this!** If you walk away from Sewall–Belmont House with one fact in mind, let it be this: Alice Paul wrote the first version of the Equal Rights Amendment in 1923, which still reads, "Equality of rights under the law shall not be denied or abridged by the United States on account of sex." This amendment passed in Congress in 1972, but to this day, it remains three states short of ratification. As inconceivable as it seems in the twenty-first century, the battle for equality is still in progress—and as you learn of the campaign led by Alice Paul, you may feel the stirring of the passion she mustered to gain incremental rights for American women.

Hours: Visitation is by tour only. Tours are given Tuesday to Friday from 11:00 A.M. to 3:00 P.M. (The last tour begins at 2:00 P.M.) On Saturday, hours are from noon to 4:00 P.M. (The last tour begins at 3:00 P.M.)

Fees: A $5.00 donation per person is suggested but not required.

How to get there: Sewall–Belmont House and Museum is located at the corner of Constitution Avenue and Second Street Northeast, next to the Hart Senate Office Building.

Metro: Union Station (Red Line). From the station's main entrance, turn left and walk past the Thurgood Marshall Federal Judicial Building to the intersection of Second Street Northeast and Massachusetts Avenue. Turn right onto Second Street. Walk three blocks, passing the Senate parking lot and Hart Senate Office Building on the right. The Sewall–Belmont House is located just beyond the entrance to the Hart building.

Metro: Capitol South (Blue and Orange Lines). Exit the station and travel on First Street Northeast in the direction of the Capitol for four blocks to Constitution Avenue. Cross the street, turn right, and walk past the Dirksen and Hart Senate Office Buildings to the end of the block. The Sewall–Belmont House is on the corner.

Stamping Locations and What the Cancellations Say
Inside Sewall–Belmont House

☐ SEWALL–BELMONT NAT'L HIST. SITE/WASHINGTON, DC ❶

National Capital Parks–East headquarters*

☐ SEWALL–BELMONT HOUSE/WASHINGTON, D.C. ❶

49 Suitland Parkway

Part of National Capital Parks–East
(202) 690–5185
www.nps.gov/nace/suitlandparkway.htm

Number of cancellations: One, plus twelve additional cancellations at National Capital Park–East headquarters

Difficulty: Easy

About this site: Today it's a dual lane parkway open to visitors and commuters, but when the Bureau of Public Roads first built Suitland Parkway in the early days of World War II, the road served as a rapid transit route between Camp Springs (Andrews Field) in Maryland and Bolling Field Air Force Base—and, ultimately, the Pentagon. To this day, the White House and congressional and military personnel still use this road as the most direct route to what is now commonly known as Andrews Air Force Base, and visiting dignitaries who fly into Andrews get their first view of Washington, D.C., from this scenic road.

Don't miss this! Considering its military origins, we wouldn't expect to find well-maintained natural habitat here, but the fact is that Suitland Parkway is lined with forests, shrubby vegetation, and wetlands that host a remarkable number of nesting bird species. Edge lands along the parkway provide pretty fair viewing opportunities for forest birds like eastern wood-pewee, Acadian flycatcher, wood thrush, red-eyed vireo, ovenbird, and scarlet tanager, and several warbler species nest in the thick foliage around Henson Creek. A flash of blue may be an indigo bunting or a blue grosbeak, and the shrubs near Andrews Air Force Base often contain ground-feeding sparrow species.

Hours: The parkway is open twenty-four hours every day.

Fees: There is no admission fee.

How to get there: Suitland Parkway begins at the Frederick Douglass Memorial Bridge (South Capitol Street Bridge) in the District of Columbia and extends 9.35 miles to Maryland 4 (Pennsylvania Avenue) at Andrews Air Force Base.

Stamping Locations and What the Cancellations Say
National Capital Parks–East headquarters*

☐ SUITLAND PARKWAY/WASH, DC/SUITLAND, MD ❶

(703) 289–2500
www.nps.gov/this

Number of cancellations: Four for the memorial, plus four additional cancellations at Arlington, and thirteen additional cancellations at Turkey Run Park

Difficulty: Easy

About this site: Our twenty-sixth president placed conservation of open spaces as one of his highest priorities, based on his own love of the wilderness and all things outdoors. His death in 1919 prompted a groundswell of interest in the establishment of this ninety-one-acre wooded island as fitting memorial to the man who created the USDA Forest Service and used the 1906 Antiquities Act to create sixteen national monuments and fifty-one wildlife refuges as the first conservation president. Roosevelt's example of environmental awareness set the pace for land preservation in the United States, and put forth a model that other nations emulate to this day. The monument itself, with its statue of TR sculpted by Paul Manship, includes four memorial tablets that state the president's views on ideals of Man, Nature, Youth, and the State.

Don't miss this! If you're walking or biking the Mount Vernon Trail (part of the Potomac Heritage National Scenic Trail in Virginia), you can reach the island from the trail, saving yourself the drive to this site. No vehicles of any kind are allowed on the island, so this is a lovely place to take a walk—and 2.5 miles of nature trails provide easy strolling through wetland marshes and woodlands. It's a treat to look back at the city, especially toward the John F. Kennedy Center for the Performing Arts across the water, but the cityscape is only one reminder that you're near a major metropolis, as the constant traffic noise and airline engines roaring overhead steal the peacefulness of this otherwise idyllic place.

Hours: The island is open daily, year-round. The ranger's hut on the island is staffed intermittently.

Fees: Admission to the island is free.

How to get there: From Interstate 95, take the U.S. Highway 1 exit heading north. Make a right onto one of the cross streets, go about 3 blocks, then go left onto Washington Street. This becomes the George Washington Parkway, taking you north past Reagan National Airport to the island.

From Interstate 495 to the north, follow the parkway past the island and under the Roosevelt Bridge. Exit at Memorial Bridge (just after stone arch) and head toward the Lincoln Memorial. Follow the traffic circle three-quarters of the way around and get back on the parkway heading north.

From downtown, take Constitution Avenue west. Follow signs to Interstate 66. This will take you across the Roosevelt Bridge. Once on the bridge, get in the right lane and take the very first exit on the far side of the river. The parking area is just beyond the bottom of the ramp.

Stamping Locations and What the Cancellations Say

Arlington National Cemetery Bookstore

☐ Theodore Roosevelt Island/Arlington, VA ⓤ

☐ Arlington House/Arlington, VA ⓤ

☐ GEORGE WASHINGTON MEMORIAL PARKWAY/ ARLINGTON, VA ⓤ

☐ LYNDON BAINES JOHNSON MEMORIAL GROVE/ ARLINGTON, VA ⓤ

☐ US Marine Corps Memorial/Arlington, VA ⓤ

George Washington Memorial Parkway: Turkey Run Park Ranger Station

☐ Theodore Roosevelt Island/Washington, DC ⓓ

George Washington Memorial Parkway: Turkey Run Park Headquarters*

☐ Theodore Roosevelt Island/Washington, D.C. ⓤ
(Note periods in D.C.)

Ranger hut on Theodore Roosevelt Island
Located on the trail around the memorial

☐ Theodore Roosevelt Island/Washington, DC ⓓ

51 Thomas Jefferson Memorial

(202) 426–6841
www.nps.gov/thje

Number of cancellations: One, plus a cancellation for the National Mall

Difficulty: Easy

About this site: Few men loom as large in the public consciousness of American history as Thomas Jefferson—author of the Declaration of Independence, the nation's third president, the man with the vision to purchase the Louisiana Territory and then send Lewis and Clark out to explore it. That's not to mention his skills as an architect, philosopher, horticulturalist, diplomat, inventor, and scientist. The likes of Jefferson have rarely been seen before or since.

His passion for a government that represents the people, for freedom of speech and religion, and for the fundamental rights of all people, make Jefferson a giant among America's founders. This memorial celebrates his life and accomplishments in an architectural style he might have chosen for himself: a domed circle that emulates the Pantheon in Rome. While the original design by John Russell Pope went through a series of modifications—some of them after his death in 1937—the spirit of the Rome-inspired design remains, reflecting Jefferson's own choices for his home, Monticello.

Don't miss this! Here's a story you won't find at the memorial: The bronze statue of Jefferson that you see here was not installed until more than four years after the memorial itself was dedicated in 1943. For three of those years, a plaster cast of Jefferson, painted to look like bronze, stood in this place. It wasn't until the end of World War II, when metal shortages came to an end and the bronze could be used for a purpose beyond military weaponry, that the final bronze statue was cast.

Hours: The memorial is open daily from 8:00 A.M. to midnight. It is closed Christmas.

Fees: Admission to the memorial is free.

How to get there: Interstates 66 and 395 provide access to the National Mall and Jefferson memorial from the south. Interstate 495, New York Avenue, Rock Creek Parkway, George Washington Memorial Parkway, and the Cabin John Parkway provide access from the north. I–66 and U.S. Highways 50 and 29 provide access from the west. US 50, U.S. Highway 1, and Maryland 4 provide access from the east.

Metro: Smithsonian station.

Stamping Locations and What the Cancellations Say
Thomas Jefferson Memorial Bookstore

☐ Thomas Jefferson National Memorial/Washington, D.C. **❶**

☐ National Mall & Memorial Parks/Washington, DC **❷**

52 Ulysses S. Grant Memorial

Part of National Mall & Memorial Parks
(202) 426–6841
www.nps.gov/nama

Number of cancellations: One, plus eighteen additional cancellations at Survey Lodge

Difficulty: Easy

About this site: General Ulysses S. Grant, America's eighteenth president, leader of the Union troops in the Civil War, and the hero who brought victory home to the North, receives recognition here as the calm, cool-headed commander his army knew him to be. This monument, a twenty-year project designed and constructed by artist Henry Shrady, stands 252 feet long and 71 feet wide. Like a moment snatched directly from the War Between the States, it depicts Grant on his warhorse, Cincinnati, while Union and Confederate troops flank him on either side.

❶ Don't miss this! You may wonder how a thirty-one-year-old artist with little previous experience won the contract to create this imposing monument, which was based on a design he submitted in a 1902 competition for the job. Henry Shrady was chosen by a panel that included the venerable Augustus Saint-Gaudens, one of the most renowned monument designers of the time (his statues and bas-reliefs grace local, state, and national parks across the country), and two of Grant's former officers, Generals John McAllister Schofield and Wesley Merritt. Clearly Shrady's design had captured the essence of Grant. The artist spent the next twenty years making his creation as representative of the man as possible. In his efforts to understand his subject from the inside, Shrady even joined the National Guard for several years to experience a soldier's life firsthand.

Hours: The memorial never closes.

Fees: Admission to the memorial is free.

How to get there: The memorial is at the base of Capitol Hill, overlooking the National Mall on First Street between Pennsylvania and Maryland Avenues.

Stamping Locations and What the Cancellations Say
Survey Lodge Ranger Station*

☐ Ulysses S. Grant Memorial/Washington, D.C. ⓞ

53 U.S. Navy Memorial

Part of George Washington Memorial Parkway
(202) 737–2300
www.lonesailor.org

Number of cancellations: One

Difficulty: Tricky

About this site: Built both to honor the men and women of the United States Navy and to aid in bringing the struggling Pennsylvania Avenue of the 1970s back to life, the U.S. Navy Memorial presents visitors with a 100-foot diameter amphitheater and plaza with a granite map of the world as its floor. Fountains and pools surround the map, providing an aquatic component to a monument dedicated to those who serve their country on the high seas. Today's visitors can enjoy Concerts on the Avenue here, a weekly series performed by the U.S. Navy Band and other service bands in the Washington, D.C., area.

Stamping tips: The U.S. Navy Memorial Bookstore, also known as the Shipstore, is closed Sunday year-round. The store is also closed on Monday during the winter months.

❶ **Don't miss this!** Don't leave the memorial without finding the Lone Sailor, perhaps the most iconic image of a U.S. Navy bluejacket in existence, standing alone with his gear and gazing ahead as if scanning the horizon for incoming ships. Created by artist Stanley Bleifeld as a composite of the qualities attributed to sailors of every age and background, the Lone Sailor holds the rank of senior second-class petty officer and displays the characteristic world-weariness of a seasoned veteran who has faced battle, gunned down enemies, and made it home alive. Artifacts from eight Navy ships were melted in with the bronze used to cast this statue, from the Revolutionary War's USS *Constitution* to the USS *Seawolf,* a modern, nuclear-powered submarine.

Hours: The memorial is open Tuesday to Saturday from 9:30 A.M. to 5:00 P.M. from November 1 through February 28, and is closed Sunday and Monday. From March 1 through October 31, the memorial is open Monday to Saturday from 9:30 A.M. to 5:00 P.M., and is closed Sunday.

From March 1 to October 31, the monument store is open Monday to Saturday from 9:30 A.M. to 5:00 P.M. It is closed on Sunday. From November 1 to February 28, the store is open Tuesday to Saturday from 9:30 A.M. to 5:00 P.M., and is closed Sunday and Monday.

Fees: Admission to the memorial is free.

How to get there: The U.S. Navy Memorial & Naval Heritage Center is located at 701 Pennsylvania Avenue Northwest.

Metro: Green and Yellow Lines stop at Archives–Navy Memorial.

Stamping Locations and What the Cancellations Say
Shipstore
701 Pennsylvania Avenue #123

☐ U.S. Navy Memorial/Washington, D.C. ⓪

54 Vietnam Veterans Memorial

(202) 426–6841
www.nps.gov/vive

Number of cancellations: Three for the Vietnam memorial. An additional four cancellations are available with the Vietnam cancellation at the Lincoln Bookshop. Eighteen additional cancellations are found at Survey Lodge.

Difficulty: Easy

About this site: More than 58,000 American lives were lost in the Vietnam War, and each and every one of their names is inscribed here on the Wall, the black granite expanse set below ground level in this peaceful position on the National Mall. Controversial from the first presentation of Maya Yin Ling's design, this memorial nonetheless attracts hundreds of thousands of people annually who walk its length, read the names, and contemplate the purpose of this attempt to protect the South Vietnamese from an encroaching Communist regime to the north.

❶ Don't miss this! Two additional memorials stand here in response to criticisms from Vietnam veterans, their families, and some members of Congress who felt the Wall did not represent the courage and heroism demonstrated by all of those who served in this war. The Three Servicemen statue more literally illustrates this spirit of patriotism and brotherhood, uniting three men in swamp-drenched clothing on the field of battle. The Vietnam Women's Memorial brings attention to an otherwise unrepresented group of people who gave their service—and for many, their lives—for the cause of democracy in Southeast Asia. Nurses saved thousands of lives while sacrificing their own comfort and facing the most horrific realities of war day after day, and the three uniformed women of this statue bring their trials and triumphs into sharp relief.

Hours: The memorial is open daily from 8:00 A.M. to 11:45 P.M.

Fees: Admission to the memorial is free.

How to get there: Interstates 66 and 395 provide access to the National Mall and the memorial from the south. Interstate 495, New York Avenue, Rock Creek Parkway, and George Washington Memorial Parkway provide access from the north. I-66 and U.S. Highways 50 and 29 provide access from the west. US 50, U.S. Highway 1, and Maryland 4 provide access from the east.

Metro: Foggy Bottom station.

Stamping Locations and What the Cancellations Say
Vietnam Veterans Memorial Information Kiosk

☐ Vietnam Veterans Memorial/Washington, D.C. ❶

Lincoln Memorial Bookshop

☐ Vietnam Veterans Memorial/Washington, DC **Ⓓ**

☐ Constitution Gardens/Washington, D.C. **Ⓓ**

☐ Lincoln Memorial/Washington, D.C. **Ⓓ**

☐ National Mall & Memorial Parks/Washington, D.C. **Ⓓ**

☐ Korean War Veterans Memorial/Washington, D.C. **Ⓓ**

Survey Lodge Ranger Station*

☐ Vietnam Veterans Memorial/Washington, DC **Ⓓ**

55 Washington Monument

(202) 426–6841
www.nps.gov/wamo

Number of cancellations: One, plus cancellations for the National Mall and National Capital Region

Difficulty: Easy

About this site: This monument, one of the most recognizable in the world, is the tallest structure in the District of Columbia for a reason: It honors our first president, George Washington, for his service in the Revolutionary War and in leading the establishment of the world's most successful democratic government. Despite public demand for a fitting tribute to Washington during his lifetime, officials did not break ground on the construction of the obelisk we see today until 1848, nearly fifty years after the president's death—and even then, construction endured many setbacks, including a funding cut that prevented its completion until 1884. Note the change in marble color 152 feet from the ground, which marks the spot where construction came to a halt in 1854; it did not resume until 1880.

Stamping tips: The only way to get these cancellations—including two that are not available anywhere else in Washington, D.C.—is to go to the top of the 500-foot monument. Happily, you do this by elevator, so the trip won't strain your heart or lungs. The monument also provides one of the all-time great views of the capital city through tiny windows in the pyramid at its crown.

During the chilly winter months, you probably won't battle lines of visitors who want to get tickets to ride to the top... but from early spring through late fall, you're sure to encounter hordes who want to make this American pilgrimage to the peak. Free tickets are distributed for each day's visit from the kiosk on the Washington Monument grounds at Fifteenth Street and Jefferson Drive. There are no reservations—all same-day tickets go on a first-come, first-served basis. Hours for the ticket kiosk are 8:00 A.M. to 4:30 P.M., but tickets run out early, and you're likely to encounter a line even an hour or more in advance of the opening time.

This American icon is one of the most heavily guarded, so don't mess with the security system or personnel—no one has a sense of humor about security in Washington, D.C. Food of any kind, beverages beyond drinking water in a clear plastic bottle, cigarettes or other smoking material, strollers, and animals have always been prohibited within the monument. In addition, be sure to leave the following items in your car or hotel room: guns and/or ammunition; knives; aerosol cans or Mace; baggage or packages larger than 18 inches x 16 inches x 8 inches. The National Park Service doesn't store items and won't hold them for you at security until you come down, so don't take a chance on getting turned away by bringing your Swiss Army knife or your backpack with you.

Don't miss this! Some of them are simple, and some are ornate, but every one of the 193 commemorative stones inside the Washington Monument came from people and municipalities who chose to demonstrate their respect for George Washington in this manner. These stones become visible when you descend from the monument's top, as the glass elevator goes from opaque to transparent in two places on the way down. Made from materials found in each individual state and showing the scars of more than a century of moisture (and, in some cases, vandalism), these stones provide a sense of nationwide participation in the creation of this stunning monument to our most famous founding father.

Hours: The monument is open daily from 9:00 A.M. to 4:45 P.M. It is closed Christmas.

Fees: Admission to the monument is free.

How to get there: Interstates 66 and 395 provide access to the

National Mall and Washington Monument from the south. Interstate 495, New York Avenue, Rock Creek Parkway, and George Washington Memorial Parkway provide access from the north. I-66 and U.S. Highways 50 and 29 provide access from the west. US 50, U.S. Highway 1, and Maryland 4 provide access from the east.

Two-hour parking is available for the monument off Constitution Avenue near Fifteenth Street, but this is very limited. Parking is available on city streets during non-rush hour times (9:00 A.M. until 4:00 P.M.) during the week. Long-term parking is available along Ohio Drive under the Fourteenth Street Bridge.

Metro: Smithsonian station.

Stamping Locations and What the Cancellations Say
Top of Washington Monument

☐ Washington Monument/Washington, DC ❶

☐ National Capital Region/Washington, D.C. ❶

☐ National Mall & Memorial Parks/Washington, D.C. ❶

56 World War II Memorial

(202) 426–6841
www.nps.gov/nwwm
Number of cancellations: Two
Difficulty: Easy
About this site: Dedicated on Memorial Day weekend 2004, this new memorial, officially known as the National World War II Memorial, celebrates the sacrifice and triumph of more than sixteen million Americans who served in World War II, including the 400,000 who lost their lives overseas in combat. At once literal and symbolic, sweeping and contained, this distinguished memorial not only commemorates those who fought and perished or those who lived to see victory, but also the people at home and their efforts to support the war through factory labor and sales of war bonds.

❶ **Don't miss this!** Symbols abound at this memorial, but visitors will have no trouble discerning the meaning in the Field of

Stars—one star for every one hundred people who gave their lives overseas—the pavilions with their eagles supporting laurel wreaths, or the images brought to life in the bas-reliefs. Most interesting, however, is that the bas-reliefs are isocephalic—a Greek term meaning that the heads of the most prominent figures in each line up along the same horizontal plane. Why is this important? Simply put, it places the emphasis on the individual, an important element in expressing the sense of unity and single-ness of purpose the United States demonstrated during the Second World War. It's hard to imagine that this kind of laser-point focus could happen again in our country, so it's particularly stir-ring to see it captured here, where it may never be forgotten.

Hours: The memorial is open daily from 8:00 A.M. to midnight. It is closed Christmas. The memorial may be secured for events celebrating Independence Day (July 4).

Fees: Admission to the memorial is free.

How to get there: The memorial is located on Seventeenth Street between Constitution and Independence Avenues, and between the Washington Monument to the east and the Lincoln Memorial to the west.

Interstates 66 and 395 provide access to the National Mall and the memorial from the south. Interstate 495, New York Avenue, Rock Creek Parkway, and George Washington Memorial Parkway provide access from the north. I–66 and U.S. Highways 50 and 29 provide access from the west. US 50, U.S. Highway 1, and Maryland 4 provide access from the east.

Metro: Smithsonian station.

Stamping Locations and What the Cancellations Say

World War II Memorial visitor center

☐ World War II Memorial/Washington, D.C. **Ⓓ**

Survey Lodge Ranger Station*

☐ World War II Memorial/Washington, D.C. **Ⓓ**

Help Us Keep This Guide Up to Date

Every effort has been made by the author and editors to make this guide as accurate and useful as possible. However, many things can change after a guide is published—trails are rerouted, regulations change, techniques evolve, and so on.

We would love to hear from you concerning your experiences with this guide and how you feel it could be improved and kept up to date. While we may not be able to respond to all comments and suggestions, we'll take them to heart, and we'll also make certain to share them with the author. Please send your comments and suggestions to the following address:

FalconGuides
Reader Response/Editorial Department
P.O. Box 480
Guilford, CT 06437

Or you may e-mail us at:

editorial@GlobePequot.com

Thanks for your input, and happy travels!

About the Author

Randi Minetor has visited more than 200 national parks, and has written several books for FalconGuides, including the *Passport To Your National Parks® Companion Guides* series and two *National Park Pocket Guides*. Randi served as a consultant and writer for Eastern National's *Passport Explorer,* the big brother to the best-selling *Passport To Your National Parks®* book. Her groundbreaking book *Breadwinner Wives and the Men They Marry* (New Horizon Press, 2002) continues to receive national media  attention, and her articles have appeared in dozens of trade magazines on subjects ranging from municipal water system management to technical theater. She and her husband, Nic, live in Rochester, New York.